Handwriting Without Tears®
2nd Grade
Printing Teacher's Guide

Guide to Multisensory Lessons and Activities for...

Handwriting Without Tears®

Name :

Printing Power

diver   sailfish   gumballs   girl

by Jan Z. Olsen, OTR and Emily F. Knapton, OTR/L

Handwriting Without Tears®

Jan Z. Olsen, OTR

8001 MacArthur Blvd
Cabin John, MD 20818
301.263.2700
www.hwtears.com

Authors: Jan Z. Olsen, OTR and Emily F. Knapton, OTR/L
Illustrator: Jan Z. Olsen, OTR
HWT Graphic Designers: Leah Connor and Julie Koborg

The Handwriting Without Tears® program and teachers' guides are intuitive and packed with resources and information. Nevertheless, we are constantly developing new ideas and content that make handwriting easier to teach and to learn.

To make this information available to you, we created a password protected section of our website exclusively for users of this teacher's guide. Here you'll find new tips, in-depth information about topics described in this guide, extra practice sheets, other instructional resources, and material you can share with students, parents, and other educators.

Just go to **www.hwtears.com/click**, and enter your passcode, **TGPP8**.

Enjoy the internet resources, and send us any input that you think would be helpful to others: janolsen@hwtears.com.

WELCOME

The Handwriting Without Tears® program continues to evolve. This *2nd Grade Printing Teacher's Guide* is the culmination of successes from previous editions, plus many new ideas from our collaborations with teachers, occupational therapists, and administrators across the country.

We appreciate all the educators who bring such drive and curiosity to making handwriting easier for children. Your feedback and ideas have helped shape this guide.

Good handwriting is one of the foundation skills of language development. It is also a skill that regularly goes on public display and one of the first observable measures of school success. With your guidance, handwriting will be an easy victory for children, enabling them to do better in school.

You can help children develop their handwriting skills so they can focus on content rather than on the mechanics of letter and number formation. As children gain handwriting mastery, their writing becomes more fluid and automatic so they can write with speed and ease in all of their classes.

If you are in a hurry, jump straight to the lesson plans for *Printing Power*, starting on page 50 of this guide. When you have time, there is a wealth of information in the earlier sections that will give you new tools and insights into the handwriting process. As you get further along and see this icon for A Click Away, be sure to visit **www.hwtears.com/click** for more program information and resources.

Please keep the suggestions coming. Your comments, criticisms, and compliments help us learn what we can do to make the Handwriting Without Tears® program work even better for students and educators.

Thanks,

Jan Z. Olsen

Emily F. Knapton

Jan Z. Olsen, OTR

Emily F. Knapton, OTR/L

INTRODUCTION

2nd Grade Printing Teacher's Guide is the guide to the student workbook, *Printing Power*. The tips and lesson plans here will help you be a great handwriting teacher. In addition to teaching posture, paper, and pencil skills, you will also teach:

- Letter skills
- Word skills
- Sentence skills

With each step, your students will easily learn what is needed to excel not only in the skill of handwriting, but also in the ability to assess their own handwriting skills. Our goal is to help students learn proper handwriting habits and then apply those habits naturally and automatically to all writing experiences.

Pay particular attention to the stages of learning:
1. Imitation (writing after a live demonstration)
2. Copying (writing from a model)
3. Independent Writing (writing without any assistance or models)

You will be amazed by what your students will learn when these skill levels are combined in well-coordinated instruction.

Aa Bb Cc Dd Ee Ff Gg Hh Ii Jj Kk Ll Mm
63 87 60 64 70 90 65 86 69 78 74 73 85

GETTING STARTED
Prepare

The Handwriting Process

Need to Review?

HANDWRITING INSTRUCTION
Choose Your Approach

Multisensory Lessons

Music and Movement...22

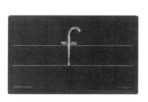

Wet–Dry–Try...24

Door Tracing...26

Imaginary Writing...28

Letter Size and Place...30

Voices...31

Mystery Letters...32

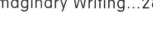

Letter Stories...34

Nn Oo Pp Qq Rr Ss Tt Uu Vv Ww Xx Yy Zz

Posture, Paper, and Pencil Skills

Why Children (and Teachers) Succeed with HWT

Printing Power

Capitals

Lowercase

HANDWRITING ADVICE

EXTRAS

Eager to start?
Lessons start here.

Printing Power

diver   sailfish   gumballs   girl

Need a schedule?
Guidelines are here.

GETTING STARTED
Prepare

ABOUT SECOND GRADE WRITERS

Times are changing. Today's second graders are expected to write more than ever. They take spelling tests, write paragraphs, do daily journal writing, and even use words to explain math problems. They need strong handwriting skills to meet these high expectations.

But what about your second graders? They come from different home and schooling experiences. Some are barely seven, and others are nearly eight. With early and late bloomers, with different English language skills, with advantaged and challenged children, you probably have quite a mix. As you get to know your students' skills, this guide will help you bring along those who are not as well prepared, fill in any missing skills for well prepared children, and develop all as capable writers. At the start of the year, you may observe reversals, awkward pencil grips, and writing from the bottom. Don't worry. Students may come to your class with handwriting problems, but you can help.

PREP YOUR SPACE...

Look at your second grade classroom. Do you have one of those modern classrooms with cafe style seating? Move those chairs and desks for handwriting lessons because children need to face the teacher to see the demonstration at the board or easel. When children face you, they hear more clearly. Ears are shaped to catch sound from the direction they face. This is so simple and amazing. Look at your class. If students are looking at you, they will see, hear, and pay closer attention.

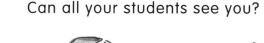

For Second Grade Children

Children come in all sizes. What about your furniture? Do the chairs, tables, and desks fit the children? The right size and style chair and desk affect school performance. One size chair will not fit every child. Check that every child can sit with feet flat on the floor and arms resting comfortably on the desk.

Can all your students see you?

Having children face you during instruction, and having children sit in the right size furniture will give your instruction and their learning an immediate boost. Now let's get your room and supplies ready for handwriting lessons.

For Demonstrations

Double Line Chart Tablet
Demonstrate on this flip chart with double lines. Children can practice on it too.

Print Wall Cards
Display the alphabet above the board to help children remember letters.

For Multisensory Lessons

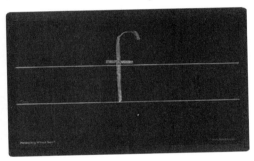

Blackboard with Double Lines
Do lowercase Wet–Dry–Try using these boards. Children can also practice spelling words and play Mystery Letter games.

Magic C Bunny
Make the puppet your teaching assistant. Your students can use him too.

Rock, Rap, Tap & Learn CD
Use the CD to make learning letters and numbers fun and memorable.

For the Children

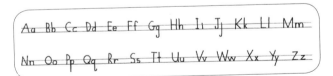

Print Alphabet Desk Strip
Place these stickers on children's desks. They help with visual recall of letters.

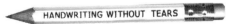

Pencils for Little Hands
Let children write with golf-size pencils that fit their hands.

Printing Power Workbook
Follow the lessons in the workbook. It's loaded with capital, lowercase, and number practice. Your students will love the fun activities that develop their word, sentence, and paragraph skills.

The Handwriting Process

THE INTENT TO PREVENT

Good handwriting skills result from your thoughtful attention and instruction. Students require deliberate instruction to develop good habits and overcome bad ones.

With this guide and HWT materials, you will be prepared to help students make writing a natural and automatic skill. You'll find that their handwriting abilities and habits vary. Regardless of where they start, you can help them develop and improve their skills:

Teach	**Fix**
How to hold the pencil correctly	Awkward pencil grips

Letters/numbers that face the right way	Reversals

3 cats

Ɛ cɒtƨ

Letters/numbers that start at the top	Starting at the bottom

top

bottom

Letters/numbers that are formed correctly and consistently	Incorrect letter/number

10 right

9 wrong

© 2008 Jan Z. Ol

PRINTING SKILLS FOR SPEED AND LEGIBILITY

You want children to write with speed and neatness while thinking about the content of their work. Would you like to know the secret of developing speed and legibility? Some people think it's practice, practice, practice that promotes speed. But practicing letters over and over actually makes letters progressively messier. Some think that trying hard is what makes printing neat. But trying hard won't work unless children have been taught properly.

The secret to achieving speed and legibility is following the simple strategies in the HWT workbooks, guides, and multisensory products. The HWT program develops eight key skills:

Memory	Name letters and numbers quickly from a random list. Visualize a letter or number quickly without seeing it.
Orientation	Print all letters and numbers without reversals.
Placement	Follow lines and place letters and numbers correctly on the baseline.
Size	Write an appropriate size for second grade. Make letters a consistent size.
Start	Start all letters and numbers at the top (except **d** and **e**).
Sequence	Make the letter parts in the correct order and direction. Make the letter parts the same correct way every time.
Control	Print the letter parts neatly—no gaps, overlaps, or extra tracings. Keep curved parts curved, straight parts straight, pointed parts pointed, etc.
Spacing	Keep letters in words close. Leave space between words in sentences.

It is clear that each of these skills is important. Children who immediately know their letters or numbers and which way they face (Memory and Orientation) don't have to stop and think. They can write quickly. Children who make their letters sit correctly on the baseline and who make them a consistent size (Placement and Size) produce neat papers. Children who always start in the right place, and make the strokes the same way every time (Start and Sequence) are able to write quickly and neatly without thinking. (Control) will come naturally as children master the above skills. (Spacing) develops from good instruction and from using the worksheets and workbooks that provide enough room to write.

Speed and Neatness

Music teachers know about speed. It's the last thing they teach. First come the notes, rhythm, fingering or bowing, and finally, practice to reach an automatic, natural level. Then pick up the tempo! It's the same with handwriting. Take a lesson from a music teacher! Work on everything else and speed will come. Children who use poor habits are doomed to be slow or sloppy. Children with good habits can be both fast and neat. That's where we are heading.

DEVELOPMENTAL TEACHING ORDER

The HWT teaching order is planned to help children learn handwriting skills in the easiest, most efficient way. It's also developmentally planned to start with a review of the easy letters: the capitals. They are the first letters children learn. Your second graders probably know them, but you want to be sure they print them correctly. The capital teaching order will help you teach:

1. Correct formation: All capitals start at the top. Strokes are made in the correct sequence.
2. Correct orientation: No reversals.

To do this, start by teaching letters in groups on Gray Blocks.

Frog Jump Capitals

These letters start at the top left corner with a big line on the left. When the first line is on the left, the next part is on the right side. This prevents reversals, while teaching good stroke habits.

Starting Corner Capitals

H K L U V W X Y Z

Reviewing these letters ensures that children start at the top left and use the left-to-right formation habit. Printing follows the same order as reading—top to bottom and left to right. This group promotes that habit.

Center Starters

C O Q G S A I T J

C O G start with a Magic C stroke. The good habits children learn here with **C O S T J** will make learning **c o s t j** much easier. There will be no problems with stroke direction or reversals.

The lowercase teaching order promotes similar success:

1. Good habits for letter formation: All lowercase letters (except **d** and **e**) begin at the top.
2. Correct placement: The tall, small, and descending letters are in proportion and placed correctly.
3. Correct orientation: No **b** – **d** confusion, no **g** – **q** confusion, no reversed letters!

To do this, the letters are taught in these groups:

c o s v w   t

The first five letters are exactly like their capitals, but smaller. What an easy start! Just bring your good habits from capitals. Lowercase **t** is made like **T**, it's just crossed lower.

a d g

These high frequency letters begin with the familiar Magic c. Starting with **c** placed correctly helps children make and place the **d** tall and **g** descending.

u i e l k y j

Here are the rest of the vowels: **u i e**. Letters **u k y j** are familiar from capitals. The focus will be on careful placement and size.

p r n m h b

They dive! They start with the same pattern: dive down, swim up, swim over! We avoid **b** – **d** confusion by separating the letters and teaching them in different groups.

f q x z

Finally **f**! Letter **f** has a tricky start. Letter **q** is taught here to avoid **g** – **q** confusion. Letters **x** and **z** are familiar, but infrequently used.

INTEGRATION: HANDWRITING AND READING

Reading and handwriting share the same symbols—the letters of the alphabet—but they require very different skills and mastery processes. Understanding these differences helps you teach both subjects well and illustrates the importance of the letter teaching order for each.

Decoding for Reading and Encoding for Handwriting

Decoding requires deciphering printed words by identifying the sounds created by the letter symbols that combine to make the word. Lessons should be focused on visual and auditory skills. The teaching order for reading uses word building to develop and reinforce decoding skills. After children master the easier sounds, they are ready to move on to the sounds that are more difficult.

Encoding requires hearing spoken language and translating sounds into letter symbols. Handwriting also requires cognitive, motor, and visual recall skills. Therefore, the lessons should be multisensory. Imitating and copying help cement letter formation habits. The HWT letter teaching order supports the development of these skills because letters are taught in groups based on similarity of formation. After children master the easier letters, they are ready to move on to letters that are more difficult to form. Teaching handwriting and reading successfully at the same time is easy, but you need to be aware of the differences.

The handwriting and reading integration options shown below work best because they adhere to the fundamental principles of each discipline and incorporate lesson work from each in a way that fully supports skill development. Find the one that works best for you.

1. Separate the handwriting and reading teaching orders

Teach both programs in the recommended orders. Keep instruction separate until familiar letters appear. Then remind children of letters they know from handwriting or reading instruction.

- During handwriting, remember reading.
  Remind students of the previously learned letter sounds.
- During reading, remember handwriting.
  Remind students how to write letters that were previously taught.

2. Integrate the handwriting and reading teaching orders

Teach both programs in the recommended order, but supplement the particular letter lesson by teaching the basic lesson associated with the other discipline.
- During handwriting, integrate reading instruction for that letter.
  Say, "We are learning to write letter **a**. Letter **a** makes the /a/ sound."
- During reading, integrate handwriting instruction for that letter.
  Say, "Take out your handwriting book. Go to the letter teaching page for **e**. We are going to do an extra handwriting lesson today to learn letter **e**." (Note: Use only the letter teaching page for **e**)

3. Follow the reading teaching order

- During reading, teach in the reading order.
- During handwriting, teach in the reading order.
- Use the handwriting letter teaching page you need. Do the word and sentence pages after all the letters have been taught.

SCOPE AND SEQUENCE OF PRINTING

The Scope and Sequence of Printing defines the content and order of printing instruction. The skills needed for printing develop as early as preschool. Although we do not teach printing formally at the preschool level, we can informally create an environment and encourage activities to help students develop the good habits they will need later. The secret is teaching skills in a way that makes learning natural and fun.

Description

Type of Instruction

Informal/Structured: A variety of activities address the broad range of letter and school readiness skills
Formal/Structured: Teacher directed activities presented in a more precise order with specific objectives

Handwriting Sequence

Pre-Strokes: These are beginning marks that are made randomly or deliberately.
Shapes: Shapes often are introduced before letters and are a foundation for letter formation skills.
Capitals/Numbers: These use simple shapes and strokes. They have the same size, start, and position.
Lowercase Letters: These are tall, small, and descending symbols with more complex strokes, sizes, starts, and positions.

Stages of Learning

Pre-Instruction Readiness: Attention, behavior, language, and fine motor skills for beginning writing
Stage 1: Imitating the Teacher: This is watching someone form a letter first, and then writing the letter.
Stage 2: Copying Printed Models: This is looking at a letter and then writing the letter.
Stage 3: Independent Writing: This is writing without watching someone or even seeing a letter.

Physical Approach

Crayon Use: Crayons prepare children for using pencils. Using small crayons encourages proper grip.
Pencil Use: Proper pencil use is necessary for good handwriting. In kindergarten, children transfer their crayon grip to pencils.
Posture: Good sitting posture promotes good handwriting. This is taught in kindergarten.
Paper Placement: When children are writing sentences and paragraphs, they're ready to angle the paper so they can move the writing hand easily across the page.

Printing Skills

Primary Skills
    Memory: Remember and write dictated letters and numbers.
    Orientation: Face letters and numbers in the correct direction.
    Start: Begin each letter or number correctly.
    Sequence: Make the letter strokes in the correct order.
Secondary Skills
    Placement: Place letters and numbers on the baseline.
    Size: Write in a consistent, grade appropriate size.
    Spacing: Place letters in words closely, putting space between words.
    Control: Focus on neatness and proportion.

Functional Writing

Letters/Numbers
Words
Sentences
Paragraphs
Writing in All Subjects

SCOPE AND SEQUENCE OF PRINTING

	PK	K	1	2
Type of Instruction				
Informal/Structured	X			
Formal/Structured		X	X	X
Handwriting Sequence				
Pre-Strokes	X			
Shapes	X			
Capitals/Numbers	X	X	X	X
Lowercase Letters	*See note below	X	X	X
Stages of Learning				
Pre-Instruction Readiness	X	X		
Stage 1: Imitating the Teacher	X	X	X	X
Stage 2: Copying Printed Models		X	X	X
Stage 3: Independent Writing		X	X	X
Physical Approach				
Crayon Use	X			
Pencil Use		X	X	X
Posture		X	X	X
Paper Placement		X	X	X
Printing Skills				
Primary Skills				
Memory	X	X	X	X
Orientation	X	X	X	X
Start	X	X	X	X
Sequence	X	X	X	X
Secondary Skills				
Placement		X	X	X
Size		X	X	X
Spacing		X	X	X
Control		X Emerging	X	X
Functional Writing				
Letters/Numbers	X Capitals/Numbers	X	X	
Words		X Short	X Short	X Long
Sentences		X Short	X Short	X Long
Paragraphs			X Short	X Long
Writing in All Subjects		X	X	X

*Children in preschool are taught lowercase letter recognition–but not writing. They may be taught the lowercase letters in their names.

STAGES OF LEARNING

Now that you understand printing skills and the role you play in developing handwriting, it will help you understand the stages of learning. Children typically learn in a developmental order. Too often, we find ourselves in such a hurry that we rush ahead. Children learn to write correctly and easily when instructions follow these developmentally based stages. You may need to review some of the pre-instructional readiness concepts below before advancing to the more formal instructional steps that follow:

Pre-Instructional Readiness (Pre-K and Kindergarten)

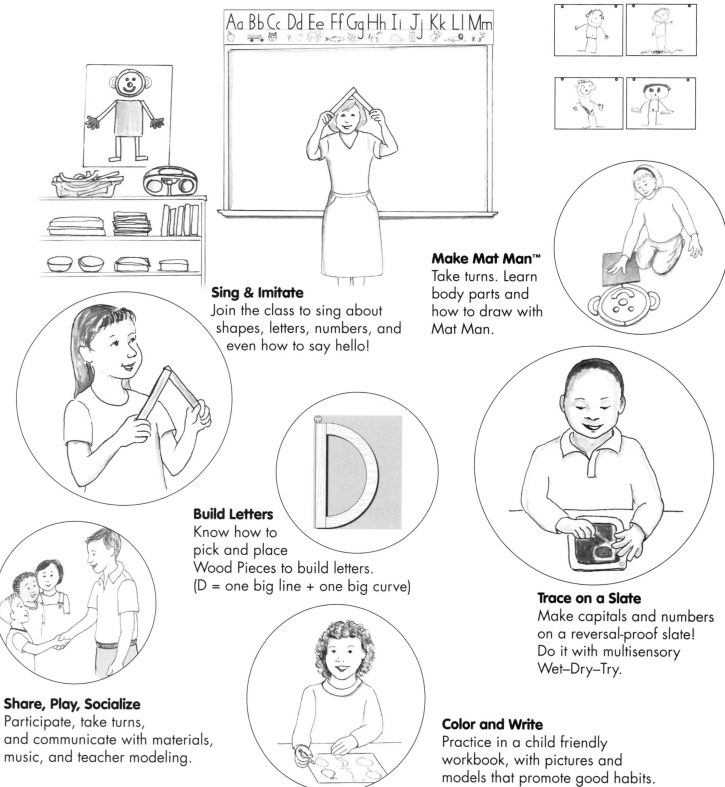

Sing & Imitate
Join the class to sing about shapes, letters, numbers, and even how to say hello!

Make Mat Man™
Take turns. Learn body parts and how to draw with Mat Man.

Build Letters
Know how to pick and place Wood Pieces to build letters. (D = one big line + one big curve)

Trace on a Slate
Make capitals and numbers on a reversal-proof slate! Do it with multisensory Wet–Dry–Try.

Share, Play, Socialize
Participate, take turns, and communicate with materials, music, and teacher modeling.

Color and Write
Practice in a child friendly workbook, with pictures and models that promote good habits.

Instructional Stages

When the pre-instructional readiness skills have been established, handwriting instruction proceeds in three stages: Imitation, Copying, and Independent Writing. Multisensory activities can enhance learning in every stage.

Stage 1 – Imitating
The child watches as the teacher writes and then imitates the teacher.

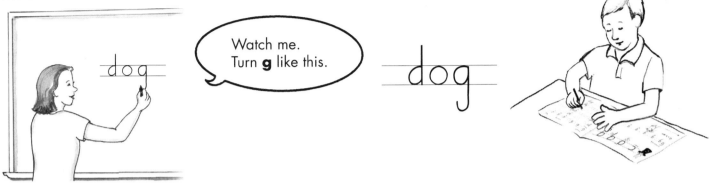

| See the motions as the teacher writes step-by-step. | Hear the directions. | See the model. | Write **dog**. |

Stage 2 – Copying
The child looks at the completed model of a letter, word, or sentence and copies it, trying to match the model.

See the model.

Write **dog**.

Stage 3 – Independent Writing
The child writes unassisted, without a demonstration or a model.

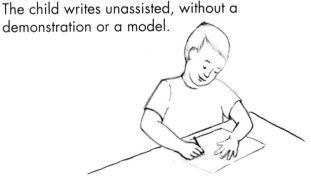

Write **dog**.

Need to Review?

The activities on the next several pages may be basic for your second graders, but they are a fun way to reinforce important teaching concepts. Skim through the next several pages to see if there is something you would like to mix into your lessons and to understand how HWT prepares younger children for success.

SHAKE HANDS WITH ME

This activity teaches right/left discrimination and an important social skill: greeting others.

Preparation

Each day, choose a different sensory stimulus (touch, scent, liquid, solid, visual, auditory).
Here are a few suggestions:
- Lotion, rubber stamp, flavoring, water in a bowl, and so forth

Directions

1. Shake hands with each child. Smile, make eye contact, and say, "Hello."
2. Say, "This is your right hand. I'm going to do something to your right hand."
   Lotion—Put a dab on the right thumb and index finger. "Rub your fingers together."
   Rubber Stamp—Stamp the right hand. "Look at your right hand now."
   Flavoring—Dab some flavoring (e.g. peppermint) on the right index finger. "Smell that peppermint."
3. Direct students to raise their right hands and say with you:
   - "This is my right hand."
   - "I shake hands with my right hand."

Skills Developed

- Social Skills—For meeting and greeting
- Right/Left Discrimination—Only the right hand is for shaking
- Directionality—A sense of directionality with the body

Tips

- Encourage children to greet others and practice shaking hands with one another.
- When you raise your right hand with your students, make sure you are facing the same direction they are.

MAT MAN™

Young children often are asked to draw pictures of themselves or a person. Mat Man makes drawing easy. The following social activities develop a child's body awareness, drawing, and counting skills. Below is an example of a child who learned Mat Man in earlier grades. Eventually she learned that Mat Man can be anyone and started to personalize her drawings of people. You can use this activity with your second graders and even help them draw other special people in their lives.

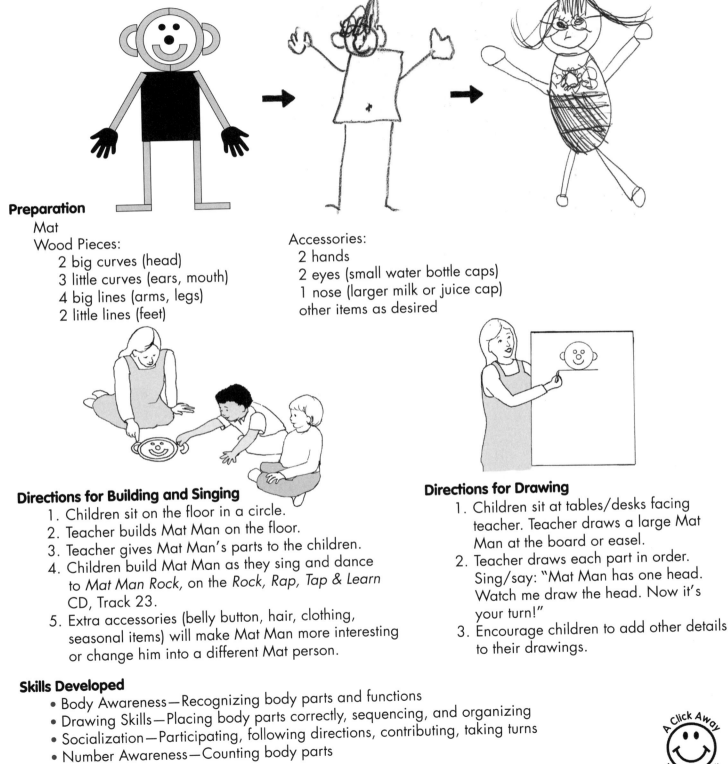

Preparation

Mat
Wood Pieces:
    2 big curves (head)
    3 little curves (ears, mouth)
    4 big lines (arms, legs)
    2 little lines (feet)

Accessories:
    2 hands
    2 eyes (small water bottle caps)
    1 nose (larger milk or juice cap)
    other items as desired

Directions for Building and Singing

1. Children sit on the floor in a circle.
2. Teacher builds Mat Man on the floor.
3. Teacher gives Mat Man's parts to the children.
4. Children build Mat Man as they sing and dance to *Mat Man Rock*, on the *Rock, Rap, Tap & Learn* CD, Track 23.
5. Extra accessories (belly button, hair, clothing, seasonal items) will make Mat Man more interesting or change him into a different Mat person.

Directions for Drawing

1. Children sit at tables/desks facing teacher. Teacher draws a large Mat Man at the board or easel.
2. Teacher draws each part in order. Sing/say: "Mat Man has one head. Watch me draw the head. Now it's your turn!"
3. Encourage children to add other details to their drawings.

Skills Developed

• Body Awareness—Recognizing body parts and functions
• Drawing Skills—Placing body parts correctly, sequencing, and organizing
• Socialization—Participating, following directions, contributing, taking turns
• Number Awareness—Counting body parts

Tips

• For second graders, demonstrate drawing arms and legs with two parallel lines.
• Encourage second graders to personalize all of their drawings.

LEARNING THE TOP!

English is a top-to-bottom, left-to-right language. That's the way we read and write. The top-to-bottom habit is the key to printing quickly and neatly. Children who start letters at the top don't have to think about making letters. They can print automatically and quickly without becoming sloppy. Starting at the bottom causes difficulty because it is impossible to write quickly without becoming sloppy. This demonstration proves the importance of starting at the top. Try it!

Make 5 lines down.   Make 5 lines, alternating down/up.   Now do it again, quickly.

↓ slow | | | | | ↓↑ slow | | | | | ↓ fast | | | | | ↓↑ fast (| \ | |

By starting at the top, you can be both fast and neat. Children who start letters at the bottom often are slow or sloppy.

Sing About It – *Where Do You Start Your Letters?*

In this guide, you'll learn how to correct bad habits and emphasize good ones with easy and fun techniques. Start by teaching this fun song. You know the tune: *If You're Happy and You Know It*. The lyrics for *Where Do You Start Your Letters?* are below. Be sure to also try our rock-n-roll version (it includes numbers too). You can find it on our *Rock, Rap, Tap & Learn* CD, Track 2. Children will have great fun singing and dancing while learning the difference between top, bottom, and middle.

Where Do You Start Your Letters?

Chords
F = C F A
C7 = C E G B♭
B♭ = F B♭ D

Where do you start your letters? At the top!
Where do you start your letters? At the top!
If you want to start a letter, then you
better better better Remember to start it At the top!

Use this song when you're teaching or reviewing PRINTED CAPITALS.

Tune: *If You're Happy and You Know It*

BASIC STROKES: SIGN IN PLEASE!

Because some letters are easier to form than others, in pre-k and kindergarten we teach pre-strokes to children based on developmental principles.*Studies show that children gradually develop the ability to copy forms in a very predictable order as shown below:

* Gessell, Arnold, and others. *The First Years of Life.* New York: Harper and Row. 1940.

Alphabet Sign-In

This activity is fun and develops many important skills. Second graders can have fun by signing in alphabetically.

Preparation

1. Prepare blackboard with a wide stop line near the bottom. (A blackboard is best, but you can use a white board.)
2. Break chalk into small ½" pieces to encourage correct grip.

Directions

1. Teacher prints **A**.
   - Write **A** up high, but within children's reach.
   - Teach **A** and each letter that follows as you write.
   - Use consistent words as you demonstrate: **A** = big line, big line, and little line.
2. Teacher asks, "Whose name begins with **A**? Adam!"
3. Adam comes to the board and you introduce him, saying:
   "This is…" (children say "Adam").
   "Adam starts with…" (children say **A**).
   "In Adam's name, the **A** makes the sound…" (children make the **A** sound).
4. Adam signs in by making a big line down from **A**. He stops on the line.
5. Repeat this exercise with each letter. Children sign in alphabetically.

Skills Developed

- Top-to-bottom letter formation
- Stopping on a line
- Names of capital letters and of classmates
- Letter sounds using classmates' names
- Big line, little line, big curve, little curve to understand the parts of each capital letter
- Alphabetical order
- Left-to-right sequencing
- Social skills including following directions, cooperating, listening, taking turns, interacting in groups
- Chalk and pencil grip
- Number concepts including counting and comparing by counting the lines for each letter.

Variation

You can change how children sign in to teach other skills:
- Horizontal line skills: underline letter from left to right
- Circle skills: circle the letter by starting at the top with a **C** stroke

CAPITALIZING ON THE CAPITALS

Teachers agree that capitals are easier, and that's where we begin. When children learn to write their capitals, they develop a strong foundation for printing. They learn important handwriting rules (such as a top-to-bottom, left-to-right habit), proper letter formation, and solid visual memory for capital letters.

Children who learn capitals first, also learn the following:
- Start letters at the top.
- Use the correct stroke sequence to form letters.
- Orient letters and numbers correctly—no reversals!

Learning capitals first makes learning lowercase letters a breeze. Think about it: **c o s v w x y z** are the same as capitals; **j k t p** and **u** are also similar to their capital partners. If we teach capitals correctly, we have already prepared children for nearly half of the lowercase alphabet.

Why Are Capitals Easier Than Lowercase Letters?

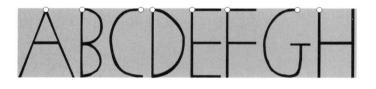

Capital letters are easy
- All start at the top.
- All are the same height.
- All occupy the same vertical space.
- All are easy to recognize and identify (compare **A B D G P Q** with **a b d g p q**).
- Capitals are big, bold, and familiar.

Let's do the math
You can see at a glance that capitals are easier for children. Students have fewer chances to make mistakes when they write capital letters. They aim the pencil at the top and get it right. With lowercase there are many more variables.

When teaching handwriting, teach capitals first. You will save yourself time, make life easier for children, and get better handwriting results.

Lowercase letters are more difficult
- Lowercase letters start in four different places (**a b e f**).
- Lowercase letters are not the same size. Fourteen letters are half the size of capitals. Twelve are the same size as capitals.
- Lowercase letters occupy three different vertical positions – small, tall, descending.
- Lowercase letters are more difficult to recognize because of subtle differences (**a b d g p q**).

CAPITAL AND LOWERCASE LETTER ANALYSIS		
	Capitals	**Lowercase**
Start	1	4
Size	1	2
Position	1	3
Appearance	• Familiar • Distinctive A B D G P Q	• Many similar • Easy to confuse a b d g p q

A PRE-PENCIL, PRE-PAPER START

Children who have used HWT in preschool and kindergarten have benefited from unique pre-pencil and paper lessons for learning capital letters. In preschool and kindergarten, children use the Capital Letter Wood Pieces to learn letter formation. We give these pieces unique names to teach capitals with consistency.

Children make letters with the Capital Letter Cards, Mat, and Slate. All have a smiley face in the top left corner. These tools help students form each letter correctly, systematically, and without reversals.

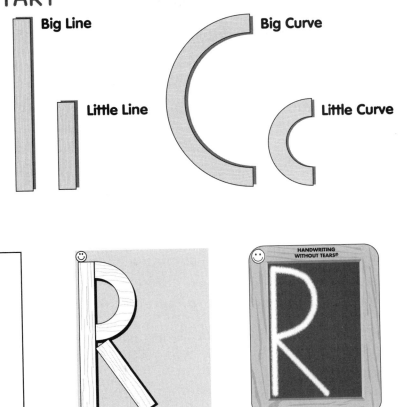

Big Line

Little Line

Big Curve

Little Curve

The Secret of the Smile

The smiley face shows that the letter is right side up and promotes the top-to-bottom, left-to-right habits.

Capital Letter Card

Mat

Slate

Teach second graders capital letter language (big line, little line, big curve, little curve) by modeling letters. Say each stroke as you demonstrate the letter. Even children who are unfamiliar with HWT concepts will learn the names quickly. The Slate is a perfect way for all your second graders to review their capitals. You only need to teach pre-k and kindergarten readiness activities if students can't remember now to form more than 50 percent of their capital letters.

Big Line   Little Curve

Little Line

Fun Review with Music

Music is a big part of our readiness curriculum. The *Rock, Rap, Tap & Learn* CD is packed with great songs that review ABCs, positional concepts, body parts, and letter formation. It's easy—the lyrics tell students what to do. You can find the song lyrics in the booklet enclosed with the *Rock, Rap, Tap & Learn* CD. The full listing of songs is on pages 22 and 23.
The circled track numbers are more suitable for review. ①

The First Grade Workbook

My Printing Book is for first graders or older students working at that level. Capital letters are reviewed. Lowercase letter lessons teach step-by-step formation and placement on lines. Activity pages put good handwriting habits to work in words, sentences, and fun activity pages. Number lessons are taught at the back of the book.

HANDWRITING INSTRUCTION
Choose Your Approach

The right approach to handwriting instruction is one that is best for you and your students. Teachers, like students, approach handwriting with different skills.

New to Handwriting Instruction?
Many teachers were never taught to teach handwriting. In fact, 90 percent of teachers surveyed say they don't feel qualified to teach handwriting. Regardless of your experience, you can be successful this year with a steady, consistent approach.

Veteran Teacher of Handwriting?
Some teachers have strong skills for teaching handwriting and assessing their students' handwriting needs. They have developed an approach that works and can easily adapt to meet individual and class differences. These teachers like to try new things and are good problem solvers. If this describes you, then you should take a flexible, varied approach to handwriting.

STEADY INSTRUCTION

You—new to handwriting, a little unsure
Your students—some with strong skills; others with weak skills and poor habits

How to Do It
1. Read this guide carefully.
    • Use the Posture, Paper, and Pencil Skill activities on pages 36-41.
2. Follow the *Printing Power* workbook page by page.
    • Review capital letters.
    • Follow a pace that suits your class for lowercase, word, sentence, and activity pages.
3. Use all the suggested multisensory lessons to support your teaching.

FLEXIBLE INSTRUCTION

You—trained and experienced

Your students—some with strong skills; others with weak skills and poor habits

How to Do It
1. Scan this guide, looking for new ideas or information.
    • Use the Posture, Paper, and Pencil Skill activities on pages 36-41.
2. Follow a flexible approach to *Printing Power*.
    • Review capital letters.
    • Review lowercase letters.
    • Teach the whole book quickly, using only the letter pages with a word or two.
    • Re-teach the whole book slowly from the beginning for word, sentence, and activity pages.
    • Integrate handwriting instruction with reading or other language arts activities.
3. Choose selected multisensory lessons to support your teaching.

Tip:
    • Don't skip Pencil Pick-Ups...all children need practice holding their pencils correctly. See page 54 of this guide.

Multisensory Lessons

Research supports the importance of multisensory teaching to address children's diverse learning styles: visual, tactile, auditory, and kinesthetic. We encourage you to include the multisensory activities in the classroom to appeal to different learning styles and make lessons more fun.

The Handwriting Without Tears® program goes beyond typical multisensory instruction. Our strategies and materials are exceptional and uniquely effective at facilitating dynamic classrooms. Here are just a few teaching methods:

Visual
- Step-by-step illustrations of letter formation give clear visual direction.
- Clean, uncluttered black and white pages are presented in a visually simple format.
- Illustrations in workbooks face left to right, promoting left-to-right directionality.

Tactile

- Wet–Dry–Try on a slate or blackboard gives children touch and repetition without boredom.
- Step-by-step workbook models are big enough for finger tracing.
- The frame of the Slate helps children make lines and keep letters and numbers well proportioned.

Auditory
- Consistent, child-friendly language helps children learn and remember easily.
- Music and different voices promote memorable and entertaining letter instruction.
- Unique Mystery Letters prevent children from using old bad habits by delaying the auditory letter cue.

Kinesthetic
- Music and movement teach letter formation.
- Door Tracing and Imaginary Writing teach using large arm movements and visual cues.

Goodbye to boring handwriting drills. Hello to fun and achievement! We assigned an interactive activity to each letter lesson. Don't be limited by our suggestions. You can use most of the activities with all letters.

Below is the list of our multisensory lessons that are described on the following pages.
- Music and Movement
- Wet–Dry–Try
- Door Tracing
- Imaginary Writing
- Letter Size and Place
- Voices
- Mystery Letters
- Letter Stories
- Magic C and Diver Letters' School*

*These lessons are specific to a group of letters and are included with the letter lessons for each group.

Tips
- Prepare ahead
- Be dynamic and silly
- Sing
- Encourage your students to participate
- Share techniques with parents
- Create your own activities

MUSIC AND MOVEMENT

The *Rock, Rap, Tap & Learn* CD is loaded with upbeat songs to make handwriting fun. The best thing about music is that it promotes movement. Whether you are teaching descending letters or spacing skills, this CD has all you need to charge up your lessons and catch your students' attention. The lyrics are on the jacket cover of the CD. The following is a list of suggested activities for each song.

Songs more suited for younger children are circled. ①

Track #	Song	Suggested Activities
①	**Alphabet Boogie**	This song will have your students doing a simple boogie to the ABCs. It is a great warm-up because it reviews the letters and sounds of the alphabet.
2	**Where Do You Start Your Letters?**	Play a question and answer game with students. Move to the song: reach to the top, bottom, and shake it in the middle. Share the song with parents.
3	**Air Writing**	Choose a letter and trace it in the air for your class. Have students follow along and trace with you. See page 28.
④	**Hey, Hey! Big Line**	Borrow kindergarten Wood Pieces to review positional concepts. All you need are the big lines.
⑤	**Diagonals**	Children learn the diagonal stroke with ease by taking an arm, reaching for the top, and sliding down at an angle.
⑥	**Big Line March**	Children will have a great time marching around with big lines. They can move, tap, and dance to this song for positional concept review.
7	**Sentence Song**	Model a sentence (no more than three words) on the board, point to the capital, the words, and the spaces in your sentence as the children sing. You can also have children write a sentence and point to the sentence parts as they sing.
⑧	**My Bonnie Lies over the Ocean**	Have your students sit or stand every time they hear a word starting with **b**. They need to listen more carefully as the song gets faster.
9	**Picking Up My Pencil**	Students learn proper pencil grip with this entertaining exercise. See page 39 for more tips on grips.
10	**Stomp Your Feet**	Students learn proper pencil grip and posture with this entertaining exercise. See page 37 for more about posture.
11	**Vowels**	This song helps students review the vowels and teaches the difference between capital and lowercase sizes.

Track #	Song	Suggested Activities
12	**Frog Jump Letters**	Children stand up and finger trace the Frog Jump Capitals in the air. Let children jump around between letter exercises. The Frog Jump Capitals are **F E D P B R N M**.
13	**Give It a Middle**	This song helps children learn the middle of **A G** and **H**. Children finger trace or watch as you model letters **A G** and **H** on the board while the song plays.
14	**Give It a Top**	Children learn about letters **T J I**. They follow you as you model these letters on the board or in the air.
15	**Sliding Down to the End of the Alphabet**	Start with **V** and slide all the way down to **Z**. This rock-n-roll song will never let children forget the ending of the alphabet. It's also great diagonal practice.
16	**CAPITALS & lowercase**	Teach letters **Cc Oo Ss Vv Ww** (easy capital/lowercase partners). Emphasize capital and lowercase sizes.
17	**Magic C Rap**	Children learn how to use **c** to make **a d g o q** with this memorable rap. See page 62 for more.
18	**Diver Letters' School**	This song incorporates movement to teach the Diver Letter group **p r n m h b**. See page 81 for more.
19	**Descending Letters**	Children will always remember lowercase **g j y p q**. Model these letters on the board. Point out that **g** and **j** go down and turn, **y** goes sliding down, **p** goes straight down, **q** goes down and makes a u-turn.
20	**Number Song**	Write numbers on paper or in the air as you use this song to review number formation.
21	**My Teacher Writes**	Use big line, little line and big curve, little curve to teach your students numbers with this interactive song.
22	**10 Fingers**	Count by tens. Five children line up side-by-side. As the chant plays children step forward and hold up their 10 fingers. Don't just stop at 50!
23	**Mat Man Rock**	Use this song to review body parts, encourage group participation, building, and counting.
24	**Head & Shoulders, Baby!**	This is a great song for warming up bodies or reviewing body parts. Children who participate will work out their wiggles and be ready to learn.
25	**Tapping to the ABCs**	The name says it all. Children can tap on their desks as they review their ABCs.

WET-DRY-TRY

We strongly emphasize placing letters correctly because it is essential for neat and fast printing. We teach on double lines because it is the easiest way to impart a sense for how letters should be placed. These Wet–Dry–Try activities on double lines are a great way to teach letter size and place. The image to the right illustrates how we discuss letter size and placement. For additional information, see pages 30 and 48. Wet–Dry–Try activities appeal to all learning styles and are a fun way to practice letters.

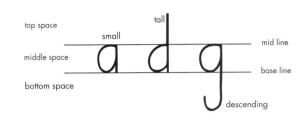

Blackboard with Double Lines

Preparation
1. Prepare Blackboards with the letter you will be teaching.
2. Place Little Chalk Bits and Little Sponge Cubes around the room so children can reach them easily.

Directions

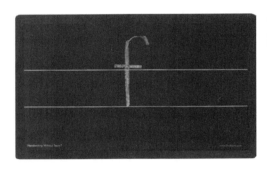

Teacher's Part
Demonstrate correct letter formation.

Student's Part

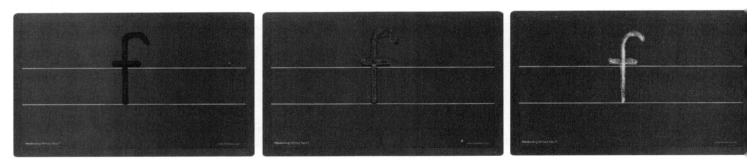

WET	**DRY**	**TRY**
• Wet a Little Sponge Cube.	• Crumple a little paper towel.	• Take a Little Chalk Bit.
• Squeeze it out.	• Dry the letter a few times.	• Use it to write the letter.
• Trace the letter with the sponge.	• Gently blow for final drying.	
• Wet your finger and trace again.		

Tips

- Use consistent words to describe the strokes. Match your verbal cues to the directions on the letter lesson pages of the workbook.
- Use Little Sponge Cubes and Chalk Bits, which help children develop proper pencil grip.
- Squeeze the sponge well or the letter will be too wet.
- This works best one-on-one or in centers with five or fewer students.
- To use this activity with the whole class, pre-mark students' chalkboards with the lowercase letter (so they have a correct model to wet), and then demonstrate once for everyone.
- To help children learn capital letter orientation and formation, use the Slate.

Other Blackboard Activities

In addition to doing the Wet–Dry–Try activity with a single lowercase letter, you can help children with bumping the lines, placing letters in words, placing capitals on lines, writing names, and more. Below are some easy, fun exercises to get you started.

Bump the Lines

Help children bump the lines with this simple dot and line exercise.

1. Use a piece of chalk to draw 4 to 5 dots with lines across the board.
2. Do the activity just as you would do Wet–Dry–Try with a letter.
3. Have children trace over the lines.
4. Say "bump" when you hit the bottom line.

Try diagonal lines and Magic C strokes too.

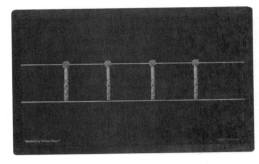

Names and Capitalized Words

Demonstrate/Imitate: Title Case (Two Boards)

1. Demonstrate the child's name on one board as the child imitates on the other.

This activity helps children learn to write their names on double lines before transitioning to paper. Practice writing capital letters and their lowercase partners on the blackboard when you teach the lowercase letter pages.

Word Skills

You can help children learn proper word spacing and letter placement.

1. Point children to the top, middle, and bottom spaces on the board.
2. You can help with word placement by preparing the board with words specific to each space. For example, the word **cows** teaches the middle space. The word **tall** teaches the top space. The word **jog** teaches the bottom space.
3. You can challenge your students by thinking of words with letters that occupy all three spaces. The word **dog** is an example.

DOOR TRACING

Take advantage of the 🙂 by placing it on the door to help children write capitals and numbers. The 🙂 prevents reversals and promotes the top-to-bottom habit.

Expanding Smiley Face Secrets

Preparation
1. Copy, color, cut, and laminate the Smiley Face on the following page.
2. Place it in the top left corner of your classroom door.

Directions
1. While teaching, use your door frame to model letter or number formation for your students.
2. Have children air trace capital letters and numbers on the door.

Skills Developed
This activity gives children extra practice with the orientation, formation, and starting position. Air tracing uses large arm movements for visual and kinesthetic learning.

Tips
Children can trace a letter or number before lunch, during recess, or before leaving at the end of the day.
- Consider having a daily or weekly leader who gets to model for the others.
- Use your door to teach parents about HWT Smiley Face secrets.
- Have students partner and play Mystery Letter games with Frog Jump and Magic C capitals.
- Play Boss of the Door. The boss gets to decide which letter or number to trace on the door. A good boss traces well enough so that others can guess the letter.

Color, Cut, Laminate, Place

IMAGINARY WRITING

Imaginary writing is a kinesthetic strategy with visual and auditory components. The picking up and holding of pencils adds a tactile component. This strategy allows you to watch the entire class and ensure that all students are making letters correctly.

Air Writing
Preparation
Learn *Air Writing*, Track 3, from the *Rock, Rap, Tap & Learn* CD.

Directions
1. Sing to prepare the class for participation.
2. Review a letter or number. Trace it in the air in front of your class.
3. Have students hold a pencil correctly in the air. Everyone checks pencil grips.
4. Retrace the letter or number again with your students.

Tip
If you are facing your students, make the letter backward in relation to you so that the letter will be correct from your students' perspective.

My Teacher Writes
Preparation
Gather chalk or markers for a large board or easel. Use *My Teacher Writes*, Track 21, from the *Rock, Rap, Tap & Learn* CD.

Directions
1. Children sing as you stand in front of the class:
   My teacher writes a letter (number) for me
   What's this letter (number) let's look and see
2. Review a letter or number and trace it in the air or on the board.
3. Have students hold a pencil correctly in the air. Everyone checks pencil grips.
4. Retrace the letter or number again with your students.

Tip
If you are facing your students and doing Air Writing, make the letter backward in relation to you so the letter will be correct from your students' perspective.

Follow the Ball

Preparation
Find a brightly colored cup or ball.

Directions
1. Have students hold a pencil correctly in the air. Everyone checks pencil grips.
2. Face the class and hold up a cup or ball.
3. Have students point their pencils at the cup or ball.
4. Write the letter in the air slowly, giving the directions.
5. Have students follow along with their pencils, saying the directions with you.

Tips
- If you are facing your students, make the letter backward in relation to you so that the letter will be correct from your students' perspective.
- Hold the cup or ball in your right hand, out to your right side at eye level. Stand still.
- Say the steps and letters, perhaps: "Magic c, up like a helicopter, up higher, back down, bump. This is lowercase **d**."

Laser Letters

Preparation
Gather a laser pointer and chalk or markers for a large board or easel.

Directions
1. Write a large letter on a board or easel, giving step-by-step directions.
2. Have students hold a pencil correctly in the air. Everyone checks pencil grips.
3. Move to the back of room, and point the laser to the start of the letter.
4. Have students point their pencils to the laser dot at the start of the letter.
5. Use the laser to trace the letter slowly, giving step-by-step directions.
6. Have students follow with their pencils, saying the directions along with you.

Note: You may decide to allow students to use the laser with your supervision.

Tips
Laser letters are ideal for teaching tricky letters because they enable children to see the following:
- You writing the large letter first
- The laser pointing to the start of the completed letter
- The laser moving along the completed letter

LETTER SIZE AND PLACE: THE HAND ACTIVITY

Teaching children the correct size and placement of letters is one of the most important things you can do to help make their printing neat and fast. The simple hand activity below is fun, gets the students' attention and is a great way to help children learn the concepts of letter size and place. Students will develop a sense for how letters fit relative to one another, enabling them to write letters the correct size and put them in the correct vertical place.

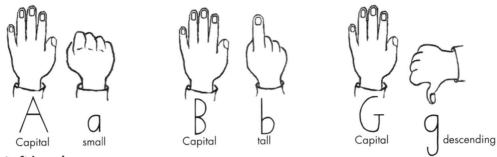

Capital · small · Capital · tall · Capital · descending

Capital letters – Left hand
- Make a flat hand for all capitals.

Capital

A B C D E F G H I J K L M N O P Q R S T U V W X Y Z

Lowercase letters – Right hand
- Make a fisted hand for small letters.
- Point the index finger up for tall letters.
- Point the thumb down for descending letters.

Small

a c e i m n o r s u v w x z

Tall

b d f h k l t

Descending

g j y p q

Directions
1. Demonstrate capitals by holding up your flat hand.
2. Demonstrate lowercase by holding up your hand for a small, tall, or descending letter.
3. Call out a letter, write it on the board, and show the hand position.

Note: Don't use this activity for children learning sign language because it may create confusion.

Directions for Hand Positions for Letters on the Board
1. Write the first lowercase letter.
2. Ask students if the first letter is small, tall, or descending.
3. Students make the right hand show the answer: small, tall, or descending. Do each letter in the word.

Alternately, write the complete word and have the class do hand positions as you say each letter.

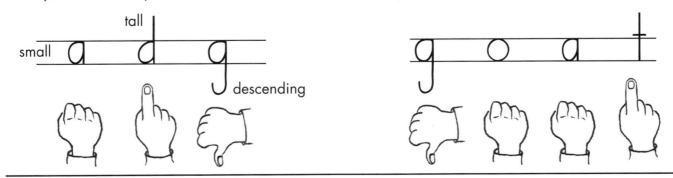

VOICES

Even with the child-friendly language in the HWT program, the steps for forming letters can get a little boring. Repeating step-by-step directions using different voices makes it fun and really helps solidify the steps in students' minds.

Preparation

1. Pre-mark the double lines on the chalkboard.
2. Begin at the far left of the board.
3. Have students open their workbooks to find the step-by-step directions for forming the letter you have chosen.

Directions

bump

Magic c   up like a   back down bump

1. Demonstrate the letter formation step-by-step.
2. Say the words that are in the workbook, and ask children to say the words with you.
3. Repeat the activity using the following voices:
   - **high**
   - **low**
   - **loud**
   - **soft**
   - **slow**
   - **fast**

Tips

- Allow your students to pick the voice for the class to use. Make it even more fun by trying voices that are spooky, shaky, robotic, etc.
- Teach with voices using the Magic C Bunny by having the bunny whisper in your ear the voice the children should use.

2008 Jan Z. Olsen

MYSTERY LETTERS

You can play Mystery Letters with children as a fun way to develop good habits. Mystery Letter lessons are for teaching correct letter formation. The secret is making the first stroke correctly before telling children the name of the letter they're going to make. This ensures that students start the letter correctly and consistently.

CAPITAL MYSTERIES

Preparation
1. Gather Slates, Little Chalk Bits, and paper towels for erasing.
2. Say the directions as indicated below.

Directions

For **F E D P B R N M**
Start in the starting corner
Big line down
Frog jump to the starting corner
Now make ____

For **H K L**
Start in the starting corner
Big line down
Now make ____
For **U V W X Y Z**
Start in the starting corner
Now make ____

For **C O Q G**
Start at the top center
Make a Magic C
Now make ____

For **S A I T J**
Start at the top center
Now make ____

FROG JUMP CAPITALS

Start in the starting corner. Make a big line down. Frog Jump back to the starting corner and finish the letter.

F E D P B R N M

Start on the dot. Copy the Frog Jump Capitals.

F E D P B R N M

MYSTERY LETTER GAME WITH FROG JUMP CAPITALS
Start in the starting corner. Make a big line down. Frog Jump back to the starting corner.
Wait for your teacher to tell you which Frog Jump Capital to make.

© 2008 Jan Z. Olsen   Handwriting Without Tears® *Printing Power* **9**

STARTING CORNER

CENTER STARTING

Play Mystery Games for Frog Jump Capitals

Play the Mystery Letter game to reinforce correct habits for Frog Jump Capitals (page 9 in *Printing Power*). The game is fun and teaches children to use correct habits. Students start at the top and don't make reversals. Here's how to play:

1. Tell students to put the pencil on the starting corner dot and make a big line down.

2. Tell them to frog jump back to the starting corner dot and wait.

3. Call out a mystery letter, one of the Frog Jump Capitals, for them to make.

Play More Mystery Games

Play the Mystery Letter game to reinforce correct habits for Starting Corner and Center Starting capitals. You can play these games on our Gray Block Paper.

Lowercase Mysteries

Preparation
1. Gather Blackboard with Double Lines, Little Chalk Bits, and paper towels for erasing.
2. Say the directions as indicated below.
3. Optional: For children who need extra help, you can make the first stroke for them to trace.

Directions
Magic C Letters

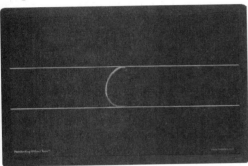

For letters **a d g o q**
Magic c, wait. Turn it into _____.

Magic C Words

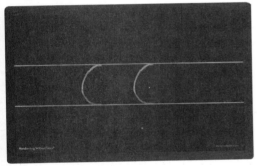

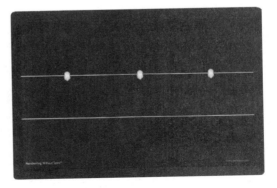

Using **a d g o q**
Magic c, wait, turn it into _____.
Add letter _____.

Turn to page 19 in *Printing Power.*
- Allow children to use colored pencils to make their letters.
- Use the Magic C Bunny to tell children the mystery letter.
- See page 66 of this guide for a list of words you can make with two or three Magic c letters.

Other Lowercase Letters

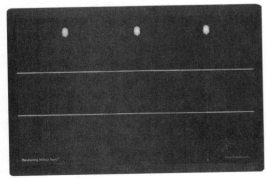

For letters **h b k l t**
Start up high, make a big line down, wait. Turn it into _____.

For letters **i j m n p r s u v w x y z**
Start at the dot. Make _____.

© 2008 Jan Z. Olsen

LETTER STORIES

Fun stories help children remember letters that are a bit tricky. Beyond our simple verbal cues, we made up some stories that are fun to share and help make these letters memorable.

b

Honeybee
Say, "Let's make letter **h**. Now let's make another **h**. I have a surprise. This is an **h** for a honeybee." Turn **h** into **b**.

e

Run the bases
Place the pencil on the dot. Say, "Batter up to bat. Here comes the pitch. Hit the ball, wait, then run the bases: first, second, third, Stop! It's not a home run."

start   hit the ball   run the bases   stop

f

Fire hose squirts
Say, "**f** is like water squirting out of a fire hose. It goes up and then falls down."

g

If George falls
Say, "Inside **g** lives a little man named George (draw a little face in **g**). He says, 'Ohhhh, if I fall, will you catch me?' Say, 'Sure, I will catch you (turn the **g** to catch George) if you fall.'"

Ohhhh, if I fall, will you catch me?

Teacher says, "Sure, I will catch you if you fall."

k

Karate K
Say, "The big line is Mr. Kaye, your karate teacher. He wants you to show him your kick. Put the pencil on the line. That's you. Now kick Mr. Kaye. Hiiii-ya. That's the karate **k**."

Mr. Kaye

you

m

Stinky m
Say, "If **m** has a big gap, people will throw trash in the gap. Don't make a big gap. Make the gap so little, there is only room for an upside down chocolate kiss."

q

U-turn
Say, "The letter **q** is followed by **u**.
Think of quiet, quit, quibble, quaint, etc.
At the bottom of **q** , stop and make a **u**-turn."

s

Stop, Drop, and Roll with S
Start **s** with a little **c**. Then what do you do if your clothes catch on fire? You stop, drop, and roll!

Go over and say hello to the smiley face.

Stop, drop, and roll.

Tt

T is tall, t is tall but...
Look at me. I can make capital **T**.
Look at me. I can make lowercase **t**.
Capital **T** is tall.
Lowercase **t** is tall, but it's crossed lower.
Capital **T** and lowercase **t** are both tall.

z

Z chase
Left hand says, "I'm going to chase you."
Right hand picks up the pencil and runs across the page. Left hand says, "I'm kidding! Come back."
Right hand slides back down toward the left hand.
Left hand says, "Ha! I'm going to chase you."
Right hand runs back across.
(This activity is for right-handers with z reversal problems, but can be adapted for lefties)

Posture, Paper, And Pencil Skills
PREPARING FOR PAPER AND PENCIL

When it comes to handwriting, children must be taught everything! That includes how to sit, position paper, and hold a pencil. This is the physical approach to handwriting. Sometimes it's the physical approach, not the letters and numbers, that causes a child to have trouble with handwriting. Think of it as playing a musical instrument. If you don't know how to position yourself and hold the instrument correctly, how can you play beautiful music? The same is true with writing letters and numbers. The ability to position yourself and hold your pencil correctly has a lot to do with being able to write legibly.

The important questions are:
- How do you get children to sit up while writing?
- How do you position the paper?
- What is the secret to a good pencil grip?

As you'll see in the next few pages...

Posture: Good Posture Can Be Fun

Does the furniture fit? The right size and style chair and desk affect school performance. Children don't come in a standard size! Check that every child can sit with feet flat on the floor and arms resting comfortably. Children who sit on their feet often will lose stability in their upper torso. On the following page we show you how good posture can be fun. We have a secret for getting children to stop sitting on their feet.

Paper: Place the Paper

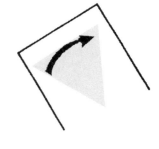

There's a misperception that people should slant their paper to make slanted writing. Not true. In fact, we slant paper so that it fits the natural arc of the forearm. Children who slant their papers properly can write faster because the arm moves naturally with the paper.

Pencil Skills: Grasping Grip

The most important thing to understand about pencil grip is that it doesn't develop naturally; it is learned. Based on our years of experience helping children, we developed our own theories about how to develop good pencil grip habits effectively. Because children are born imitators, demonstration will lead to success.

On the next few pages, we explain fun strategies to help you teach posture, paper, and pencil skills.

GOOD POSTURE CAN BE FUN

Arms and Hands

Here are some warm-ups that children enjoy.

Push palms

Pull hands

Hug yourself tightly

Total Posture – Stomp!

Stomping is fun and really works! Students' feet will be on the floor and parallel in front of them. The arm movements make their trunks straight. The noise and chaos let them release energy, but it's under your control. When you have them stop stomping, they'll have good posture and be ready to pay attention. Use stomping a few times a day.

Directions

1. Sit down and show the children how to stomp their feet and wave their arms in the air.
2. Have them shout, "Na, na, naaah, na, na, naaah," with you as they wave and stomp.

The Stomping Game

Use *Stomp Your Feet*, Track 10, from the *Rock, Rap, Tap & Learn* CD.

Directions

1. Children push their chairs away from their desks to get ready.
2. Sing and follow along with the music and movement.

Head and Shoulders

Do this activity any time you find your children sagging.

Raise shoulders up

Pull shoulders back

Let them down

PLACE THE PAPER

Where's the paper? Most children naturally place a bowl of ice cream in front of them. They may, however, lean way over in awkward positions to write. Children who put their paper in front of them and slant it properly can write faster because they position their arms naturally with the paper. You need to teach them how to place their papers appropriately. Have your students turn to page 6 in *Printing Power*, and teach them how to slant their papers appropriately for their handedness.

Children who are able to print sentences across the page are ready to tilt the paper at a slight angle to follow the natural arc of the writing hand. The correct way to tilt the paper is easy to remember (see the illustrations below). For right-handed children, put the right corner higher; for left-handed children, put the left corner higher. The writing hand is below the line of writing. This practice encourages the correct neutral wrist position.

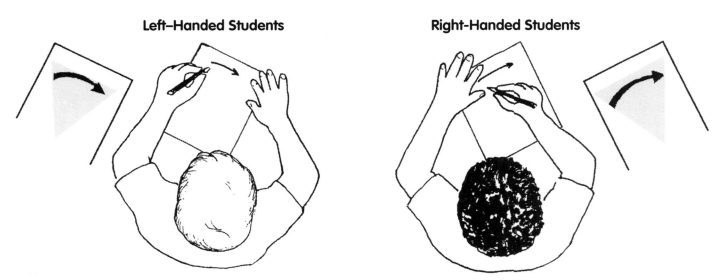

Left–Handed Students **Right-Handed Students**

- **Left–Handed Children** tend to exaggerate the position of their papers. It helps them see their writing. For more information on left-handed children, turn to page 42.
- **Beginners** who are learning to print letters and words should place the paper straight in front of them.

Tip
- Sometimes children need reminders about how to place their paper. Draw an arrow on the bottom corner (bottom left corner for right-handed children, bottom right corner for left-handed children). Tell them to point the arrow to their belly button.

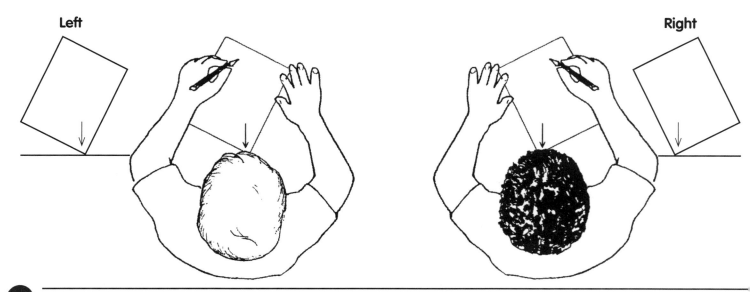

Left **Right**

GRASPING GRIP

Educators all have questions about pencil grip. We are frequently asked why awkward pencil grips happen and how to correct them. We seldom hear about how to prevent them. A good pencil grip does not develop naturally. In fact, several factors affect how a child learns to hold a pencil correctly.

Below is our top 10 list of the things we often think about regarding grip:

Experiences

We develop pencil grip habits while we are young. Children who are encouraged to feed themselves have more fine motor experiences than those who are spoon fed. Children who have early self-feeding experiences may have an easier time learning how to hold their crayons and pencils.

Toys

Today's toys are very different from those with which we grew up. We should always encourage and remind parents about the non-battery operated toys because they help build hand strength.

Imitation

Children are born imitators. When they are watching you write, always demonstrate a correct grip because they tend to do as you do.

Early Instruction

Help children place their fingers. Teach preschoolers and kindergartners their finger names and finger jobs and show them how their fingers should hold writing tools.

Tool Size

Choose appropriate writing tools. We prefer small tools: Little Sponge Cubes, Little Chalk Bits, FLIP Crayons™, and Pencils for Little Hands. These tools promote using the finger tips naturally. Large tools elicit a fisted grip; small tools, a more mature grip. As adults, we write with pencils that are in proportion to our hands. Shouldn't children do the same?

Timing

It is difficult to correct the grips of older children because we have to re-teach them motor patterns. Old habits die hard. Older children need time to get used to a new way of holding a pencil. It takes repetition, persistence, and practice. See page 41.

Blanket Rules

Avoid blanket rules about pencil grip devices. Some devices may work for a child. If they motivate and work, use them. You should save these devices as a last resort and use them for older children who understand their purpose.

Acceptance

Some awkward pencil grips are functional. If the child is comfortable and doesn't have speed or legibility issues, let it go.

Joints

We are all made differently. Some of us have joints that are more relaxed. Therefore, expect slight variations in what would be considered a standard grip. If a child is unable to use a standard grip, you may consider an altered grip as illustrated. The pencil is placed between the index and middle fingers.

Summer

This is the perfect time to change an awkward grip. Take advantage of the child's down time to create new habits.

The Correct Grip

The standard way for children to hold their pencil is illustrated below. If you write using a grip that is different than tripod or quadropod, alter your grip for classroom demonstration.

Tripod Grip
Thumb, Index Finger, Middle Finger

Quadropod Grip
Thumb, Index Finger, Middle Finger, Ring Finger

A Note About Pencil Size

We start by using golf size pencils in kindergarten and first grade. As children gain handwriting experience, their control will improve. By second grade, children should be using a standard size pencil.

Sing - *Picking Up My Pencil*

Use this song from the *Rock, Rap, Tap & Learn* CD to make your pencil grip lessons more memorable. Children will know the tune *Baby Bumble Bee*. You sing the first verse; they'll join in the second.

Directions
1. Listen to Track 9 as background music a few times with your students.
2. For fun, review the names of the fingers thumb, pointer, and tall man (middle finger).
3. Without the CD, sing and demonstrate verse one.
4. Children will then get ready by picking up their pencils, checking their own and their neighbor's grip, and joining you to sing the second verse.

*The fast pace of the song is to encourage teachers and children to pick up the tune quickly and to inspire them to sing it on their own.

The tips shown here will help your students hold the pencil with the right combination of mobility and control. These exercises make it easy and fun for children to learn a correct pencil grip.

A-OK

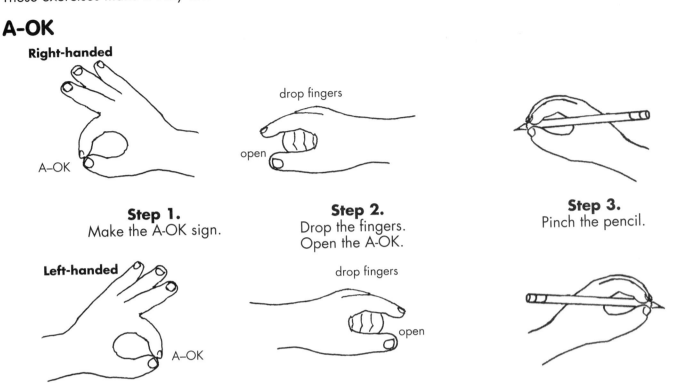

Right-handed

A–OK

drop fingers

open

Step 1.
Make the A-OK sign.

Step 2.
Drop the fingers.
Open the A-OK.

Step 3.
Pinch the pencil.

Left-handed

A–OK

drop fingers

open

Flip the Pencil Trick

Here is another method. It is a trick that someone introduced to us at a workshop. It's such fun that we love to share it. Children like to do it, and it puts the pencil in the correct position. (Illustrated for right-handed students.)

Place the pencil on table pointing away from you. Pinch the pencil on the paint where the paint meets the wood.

Hold the eraser and twirl the pencil around.

Voila!
Correct grip.

Changing Grip

There's no way of knowing for sure why non-standard grips occur. However, we believe that early instruction and good demonstration can help prevent awkward grip. Asking a child to change his or her grip is like moving something in your house after months or years of having it in the same place. What happens? You automatically go to where the object used to be. Changing habits takes time. The same is true for pencil grip. But with grip, the adjustment takes longer. Pencil grips in older children can be changed, but it takes cooperation by the child, involvement at home and school, and a lot of time. See page 128 of this guide for ways to correct grip in three easy steps.

You may also try:
1. Using an adaptive device: With older children these devices are motivating.
2. Talking to the child: If the grip is causing discomfort, the child may be motivated to change.
3. Using an incentive program: sometimes this motivates the child to break their habit.
4. Trying an alternate grip: showing children something different to spark interest.
5. Making the change over summer when the non-standard grip isn't being used.

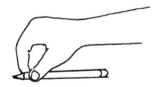

LOOKING OUT FOR LEFTIES

Many wonder if left-handed children require different instruction than right-handed child. The truth is, you instruct them the same way, with a few exceptions. Because our world typically favors the right-handed population, worksheets and letter sequence charts usually don't make special considerations. We have tips for teaching left-handed children that will prevent bad habits and make handwriting easier.

Preventing a Poor Wrist Position

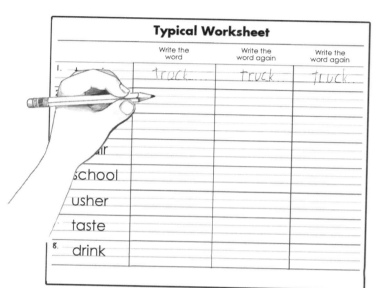

The child can't see a model.

Child accommodates but ends up in a bad position.

Many worksheets list things on just the left side. Left-handed children struggle with this format because their hand covers the thing they are attempting to copy. To accommodate their situation, some left-handed individuals will hook their wrist to see what it is they are supposed to write. After a while, the movement becomes so automatic that some children develop a natural hooked wrist pattern. This type of writing can be uncomfortable and tires children.

You can prevent this problem by photocopying the child's worksheet/workbook page and placing it to the right for the child to reference for copying.

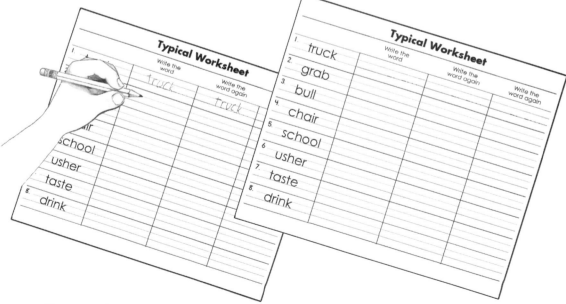

Give another copy of the worksheet to the child so the model can be seen.

Left-Hand Friendly Worksheets

When creating your own worksheets, you can make them right- and left-hand friendly in two ways:

1. Have the child copy below the model.

2. Place the word to be copied in the middle of the page.

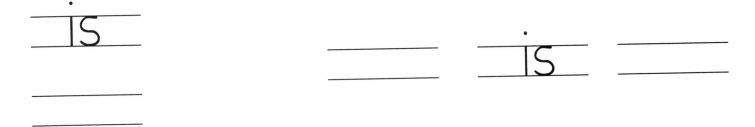

Paper Placement

You might observe some left-handed children slanting their papers too much. They do this to prevent their wrists from hooking. You can allow them to exaggerate the slant on their papers if it doesn't cause speed or neatness trouble.

Cross Strokes

Mark arrows → for right-handed students. Mark arrows ← for left-handed students.

When writing letters and numbers, we typically travel top to bottom, left to right. At times, left-handed children will choose to pull into their writing hand from right to left. Allow left-handed children to cross by pulling into their hand. Model it for them in their workbooks.

Why Children (and Teachers) Succeed with HWT

HWT LETTER AND NUMBER STYLE

HWT uses a simple, continuous, vertical stroke that is easy to learn. The HWT letter style is also familiar because it looks like the letters and words children see and read every day. The continuous stroke style prevents reversals and prepares children for a smooth transition to cursive.

Aa Bb Cc Dd Ee Ff Gg Hh Ii Jj Kk Ll Mm
Nn Oo Pp Qq Rr Ss Tt Uu Vv Ww Xx Yy Zz
1 2 3 4 5 6 7 8 9

Advantages of the HWT Style

- Follows developmental principles
- Enables ease of reading and writing
- Prevents reversals
- Looks and feels child friendly
- Features letter models with an appealing, handwritten quality

Vertical print uses 4 simple shapes.
1. Vertical lines
2. Horizontal lines
3. Circles and curves
4. Diagonal lines

Slanted print uses 12 different strokes.
Slanted print is difficult to describe and developmentally more difficult to master.

Vertical print is simple and straight.

Not Reversible

Slanted print has tails or fancy endings.
With tails, these letters are asymmetrical, leading to more reversals.

Reversible

What is it?
Is it an **i**?
Or a reversed **j**?

Vertical print is neater and holds up better in use. There is no advantage to using a slanted style for printing. Despite claims to the contrary, slanted print does not make the transition to cursive easier. The HWT continuous stroke style is ideal for printing and transitioning to cursive.

UNIQUE WORKBOOK FEATURES
Large Step-By-Step Illustrated Directions
It is so much easier for children to understand how to form letters if you show them how step-by-step. Other programs show a completed letter with a bunch of tiny arrows pointing the way around the letter. It is very difficult for a child to learn how to write that way. Step-by-step is the way to letter formation success.

Magic c   up like a   up   back down
                                 higher   bump

Child-Friendly Consistent Terminology
HWT's child-friendly language evolved in response to other programs' complicated letter terminology. When teaching letters to children, HWT doesn't assume they fully understand left/right orientation, clockwise/counter clockwise, or forward/backward. That complex terminology is confusing and unnecessary. HWT makes it easy by using fewer words and only words that children already know and understand.

HWT is simple for children to comprehend.

HWT Language:
Magic c
up like a helicopter
up higher
back down
bump

Take a look at what other programs say to form **d**:

Example 1:
Middle start; around down, touch, up high, down, and a monkey tail.

Example 2:
Touch below the midline; circle back (left all the way around). Push up straight to the headline. Pull down straight to the baseline.

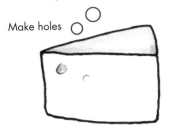

Make holes

Pencil Pick-Ups Encourage Grip Practice
Pencil Pick-Ups are designed to encourage children to hold their pencils correctly while doodling. They are a perfect warm-up activity that enables teachers to teach and check pencil grip. The Pencil Pick-Ups are on page 7 of *Printing Power*.

Capitals in Gray Blocks
Gray Blocks and starting dots help children control the size and shape of their capitals. Gray Blocks also prevent reversals. Here's how:

F E D P B R N M H K L start on the dot in the top left (starting corner) with a big line down. When that line is on the left side, the next part is always on the right side. No reversals!

U V W X Y Z start in the starting corner, too.

The dot in the top center is the place to begin:
C O Q G S A I T J
Starting at the top is the most important handwriting habit. The dot at the top teaches children to begin there automatically.

Copy Just One Model at a Time

Have you seen papers or workbooks that require children to copy a letter over and over across the page? The child copies the model and then copies the copy of the model, and so on. The letters get progressively worse. It's boring. Ideally, the child should make just one letter beside each model.

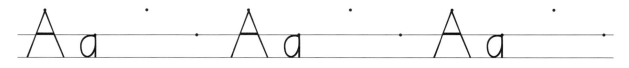

Continuous Meaningful Review

Children retain skills better if they have continuous, meaningful review. That's why each new letter is used in words and sentences that emphasize practice of the new letter and help children review and practice previously learned letters.

Room to Write

When children are learning to print, they need extra room to write. Because they can't print with the precision of machines, they cram their words to make them fit into spaces that are too small. HWT workbooks give them the room they need to write.

HWT models good spacing and gives plenty of room to help children develop good spacing habits.

Todd saws. I saw wood too.

Other programs give poor spacing models and not enough room to write. Children are expected to make letters with the precision of a professional graphic designer at a keyboard.

Example 1:

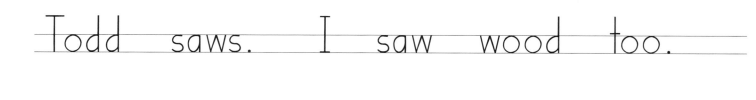

How many threes equal nine?

Example 2:

Bob's bicycle has a bell.

Left-Hand Friendly Design

The HWT workbooks are left-hand friendly. Every page places the models so that left-handed children can easily see the model they are copying. Lefties never have to lift their hands or place them in an awkward position to see a model. We give models on the right side so that when a left-handed child's arm covers the left aligned models, they can still see a model to copy.

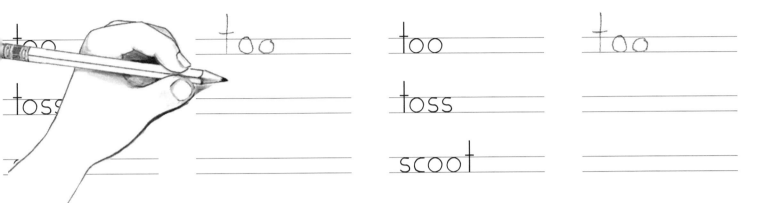

Simple Black-and-White Pages

Our workbooks have black-and-white pages that are clean and clear. We deliberately avoid the visual confusion of distracting background images, overdone colored graphics, multicolored lines, and crowded pages. These fancy effects can create visual perception difficulties for children and distract them.

The simple workbook pages keep children happy and occupied. Children who finish ahead of others can color the pictures or add drawings to the pages.

Children enjoy seeing their own writing and coloring or drawing on the pages. They like the handwritten models, which look more like their own writing. Our workbooks celebrate the child's work.

Left-to-Right Directionality

This is an exciting, unique feature of the HWT workbooks. Look at our illustrations. They promote left-to-right directionality. The dog, submarine, fish, and other drawings are going left to right across the page to encourage correct visual tracking and writing direction.

Fair Practice

In the workbooks, we never ask the child to copy or use a letter that has not yet been taught. The words and sentences use only the letters that the children already know. Using unfamiliar letters for instructional practice is unfair and causes children to develop bad habits.

Teaching Reversal Free Numbers

We begin by teaching numbers with the Gray Blocks, which are like pictures of the Slate Chalkboard. The Gray Blocks prevent reversals and help children learn to place the numbers. Our simple numbers and teaching strategies produce numbers that are reversal-proof.

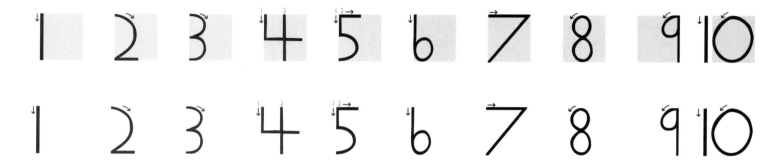

- We teach the numbers in numerical order.
- **1 2 3 4 5 6 7** begin in the top left (starting) corner.
- **8** starts at the top, but in the center.
- **9** starts at the top, but in the right corner.
- **10** is made with **1** and **O** (Number **O** and letter **O** are made the same way.)

Each number page also gives a review of previously learned numbers. The children practice writing numbers on Gray Blocks and on a single line.

Double Lines and Other Lines

With so many lines and so many styles, children need paper that will prepare them for it all. HWT Double Lines teach children to place letters correctly and naturally. With just two lines, children understand quickly how to place letters. Small letters fit in the middle space. Tall letters go into the top space. Descending letters go into the bottom space. Later students can apply that philosophy to other styles of paper they'll get in school. We also give them practice with other lines along the way.

Take a look at space.

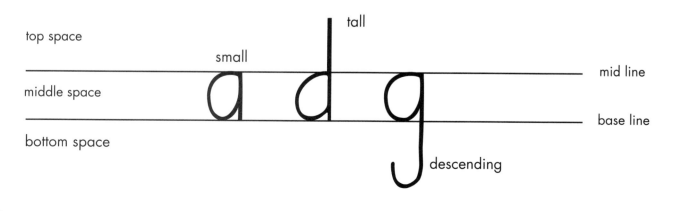

Line Generalization: Success on All Paper Styles

Throughout *Printing Power*, we provide activities for children to experience different types of lined paper. Practice using simple double lines makes it easy for students to succeed on any style of paper.

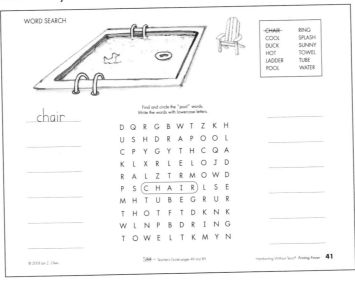

Line Generalization Success!

This child's sample shows line transition skills from HWT double lines to a journal entry with triple lines.

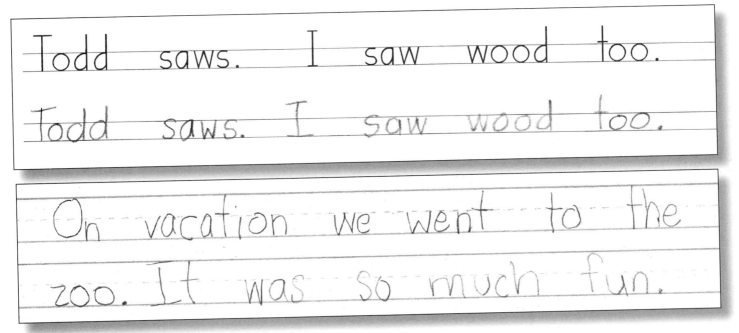

Paper

Who would have thought that the quality of paper could affect handwriting? We tested all kinds of paper, and we know good paper when we see it. Our handwriting paper is selected based on the following qualities:

1. **Writability** – This is referred to as tooth. When paper has good tooth, you can actually hear the pencil. Paper with tooth gives children feedback and assists with control. Smooth paper doesn't have tooth. It is hard to write on.

2. **Erasability** – Nothing is worse than paper that won't erase or paper that wrinkles and tears. Sturdy paper withstands erasing.

3. **Opacity** – We have the thickest sheets with the most opacity to reduce the amount of see through.

4. **Brightness** – Our paper is white. This paper helps a child's work stand out.

Printing Power
WHAT'S IN THE WORKBOOK

Printing Power places emphasis on writing words so that fluency and speed improve. Activity pages throughout the book provide review and practice opportunities, reinforcing important language arts skills.

Letter and Word Pages

- Pages show large step-by-step instructions for letter formation.
- ☑ Check letter and ☑ Check word teach children to self-edit their work.
- Capitals are reviewed.
- Newly taught letters are immediately incorporated in word practice.

Sentence and Paragraph Pages

- Newly taught letters are used in practice sentences that make up paragraphs.
- Good spacing is modeled.
- ☑ Check sentence teaches children self-editing skills.

Activity Pages

CAPITALS, COMMAS

Copy lists.

Names: Ava, Bea, Kate, Sadie, Zoe

Names:

Names: Bill, David, Jose, Mike, Nate

Names:

Cities: Bogota, Osaka, Seoul, Toledo

Cities:

States: Hawaii, Iowa, Alaska, Nevada

States:

28 Handwriting Without Tears® *Printing Power*   © 2008 Jan Z. Olsen

POEM

Apostrophe

I can spell doesn't and don't

I can spell wasn't and won't

But please, please, don't ask me

To spell apostrophe.

© 2008 Jan

THANK YOU LETTER
Write your own thank you letter.

Date

Greeting

Dear

Body

Thank you

Closing

Sincerely,

Signature

© 2008 Jan Z. Olsen   Handwriting Without Tears® *Printing Power* **67**

- Pages reinforce other language arts activities while promoting meaningful practice.
- Children learn to write sentences, poems, dates, letters, and days of the week.
- Children learn to write on paper with different line styles.
- Lessons are fun and engaging for students.

Number Pages

3 starts in the starting corner.
3 makes a little curve to the middle.
3 makes another little curve to the bottom corner.

HANDWRITING WITHOUT TEARS

three wheels

I can write 3.

3 3 3 3 3

Copy the sentences.

A tricycle has three wheels. Tri means three.

I can count to 3.

1 2 3   1 2 3   3+0= ___   5-2= ___

___ ___ ___   ___ ___ ___   4-1= ___   2+1= ___

© 2008 Jan Z. Olsen   Handwriting Without Tears® *Printing Power* **77**

NUMBER PRACTICE

Add:

$0 + 1 =$ ___ $1 + 1 =$ ___ $2 + 1 =$ ___ $3 + 1 =$ ___ $4 + 1 =$ ___

Subtract:

$7 - 1 =$ ___ $8 - 1 =$ ___ $9 - 1 =$ ___ $10 - 1 =$ ___ $11 - 1 =$ ___

Add:

$\begin{array}{c}0\\+1\\\hline\end{array}$ $\begin{array}{c}1\\+1\\\hline\end{array}$ $\begin{array}{c}2\\+1\\\hline\end{array}$ $\begin{array}{c}3\\+1\\\hline\end{array}$ $\begin{array}{c}4\\+1\\\hline\end{array}$ $\begin{array}{c}5\\+1\\\hline\end{array}$ $\begin{array}{c}6\\+1\\\hline\end{array}$ $\begin{array}{c}7\\+1\\\hline\end{array}$ $\begin{array}{c}8\\+1\\\hline\end{array}$ $\begin{array}{c}9\\+1\\\hline\end{array}$

Subtract:

$\begin{array}{c}2\\-1\\\hline\end{array}$ $\begin{array}{c}3\\-1\\\hline\end{array}$ $\begin{array}{c}4\\-1\\\hline\end{array}$ $\begin{array}{c}5\\-1\\\hline\end{array}$ $\begin{array}{c}6\\-1\\\hline\end{array}$ $\begin{array}{c}7\\-1\\\hline\end{array}$ $\begin{array}{c}8\\-1\\\hline\end{array}$ $\begin{array}{c}9\\-1\\\hline\end{array}$ $\begin{array}{c}10\\-1\\\hline\end{array}$ $\begin{array}{c}11\\-1\\\hline\end{array}$

© 2008 Jan Z. Olsen   Handwriting Without Tears® *Printing Power* **85**

- Numbers are reviewed in Gray Blocks to prevent reversals.
- Fun stories accompany most numbers.
- Review pages are functional and provide math skill practice.

WHAT YOU WILL TEACH...

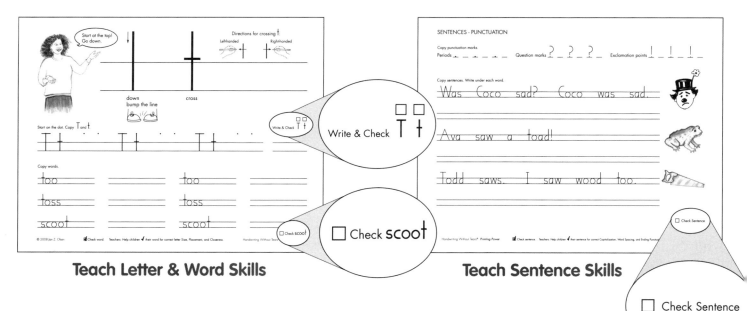

Teach Letter & Word Skills   **Teach Sentence Skills**

Letter Skills

Children need to know exactly how to make letters. Teach them and tell them:

1. Start correctly.
2. Do each step.
3. Bump the lines.

When you check students' workbook letters, explain to them what they did right and help them correct any mistakes. After you have done this a few times, students will begin to self-check with confidence.

Word Skills

There are three steps to writing words well:

1. Make letters the correct size.
2. Place letters correctly – tall, small, or descending.
3. Put letters close.

Use the Hand Activity, page 30 of this guide, to help children understand letter size and placement.
How close should the letters be? Very close, but not touching. Have children put their index fingers very close together, but not touching. That close!

Sentence Skills

Sentences must:

1. Start with a capital.
2. Put space between words.
3. End with . ? or !

This is easy and fun. There's even a *Sentence Song*, Track 7, on the *Rock, Rap, Tap & Learn* CD. Sing it to *Yankee Doodle*.

...AND HOW THEY WILL CHECK

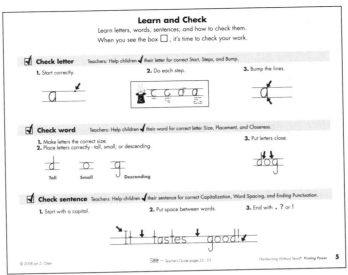

Learn and Check

Learn letters, words, sentences, and how to check them.
When you see the box ☐, it's time to check your work.

☑ **Check letter** Teachers: Help children ✓ their letter for correct Start, Steps, and Bump.

1. Start correctly.   **2.** Do each step.   **3.** Bump the lines.

☑ **Check word** Teachers: Help children ✓ their word for correct letter Size, Placement, and Closeness.

1. Make letters the correct size.   **3.** Put letters close.
2. Place letters correctly - tall, small, or descending.

Tall   Small   Descending

☑ **Check sentence** Teachers: Help children ✓ their sentence for correct Capitalization, Word Spacing, and Ending Punctuation.

1. Start with a capital.   **2.** Put space between words.   **3.** End with . ? or !

It tastes good!

© 2008 Jan Z. Olsen   S&B — Teacher's Guide pages 52 - 53   Handwriting Without Tears® *Printing Power*   5

☑ Check letter Teachers: Help children ✔ their letter for correct Start, Steps, and Bump.

1. Start correctly.

2. Do each step.

3. Bump the lines.

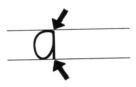

☑ Check word Teachers: Help children ✔ their word for correct letter Size, Placement, and Closeness.

1. Make letters the correct size.
2. Place letters correctly—tall, small, or descending.

3. Put letters close.

Tall   **Small**   **Descending**

☑ Check sentence Teachers: Help children ✔ their sentence for correct Capitalization, Word Spacing, and Ending Punctuation.

1. Start with a capital.   **2.** Put space between words.   **3.** End with . ? or !

It tastes good.

WARM-UPS

Teach Pencil Pick-Ups

Get Started   Say, "Turn to page 7. We are going to warm-up our fingers and practice holding our pencils. Let's pick up our pencils (walk around the room and check grips). I'm checking your fingers, now drop them and let's do it again (check grips again). Choose a picture on the page that you want to finish."

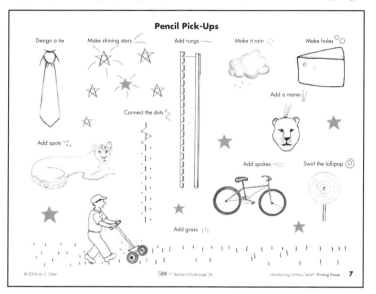

Multisensory Activities

Music and Movement
Use the *Rock, Rap, Tap & Learn* CD.
Play *Picking Up My Pencil*, Track 9.
See page 22 of this guide.

About this Page
Holding the pencil correctly is a good habit that will serve your children for years. Even if they come with awkward or inefficient grips, you can help them build new habits this year. This page will help you.

Tell them...
This is such is a funny page. There's so much to do. Do you see something you'd like to do? Put whiskers on the lion? Put spokes on the bicycle? This pencil pick-up page has fun things to do. We are going to do a little bit on this page today, tomorrow, and for many days.

How do I teach this?
Prepare for this page by helping children find the grip that suits them on page 6 of the workbook.
   1. First identify which hand is the writing hand — left or right.
   2. Then decide which grip is to be used — tripod or quadropod.
   3. Have children mark the illustration on page 6 that is correct for them.
        - Circle it
        - Color it
Demonstrate on the board a few sample strokes: Rungs, spokes, grass, or holes.
Do a two-step lesson over a period of several days:
   1. Pick up a pencil and hold it in the air to check that it's the correct grip.
   2. Make marks for just a few seconds—about 5—then stop, drop the pencil, and repeat.
Go on to a lesson page now.

CAPITALS

Teach Frog Jump Capitals F E D P B R N M

Get Started   Say, "Turn to page 8 and 9. These are the Frog Jump Capitals. See how the frog made capital **F**. We are going to write Frog Jump Capitals."

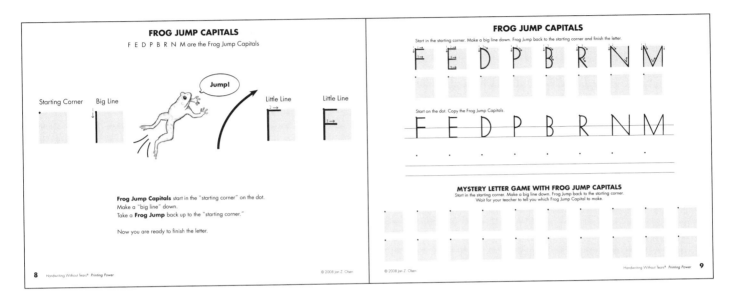

Multisensory Activities

Music and Movement
Use the *Rock, Rap, Tap & Learn* CD, *Frog Jump Letters*, Track 12. While standing, finger trace Frog Jump Capitals in the air. Let children jump between the letters. See page 23 of this guide.

Mystery Letter on the Slate
Play the Mystery Letter game. See page 32 of this guide.

Teach Letters Step-by-Step

1. Copy the capitals in the Gray Blocks. Begin on the dot.
   Follow the directions below for each letter.
   Eight capitals are Frog Jump Capitals.

F	Big line down, frog jump!	Little line across top, little line across middle
E	Big line down, frog jump!	Little line across top, middle, bottom
D	Big line down, frog jump!	Big curve to bottom corner
P	Big line down, frog jump!	Little curve to middle
B	Big line down, frog jump!	Little curve to middle, little curve to bottom
R	Big line down, frog jump!	Little curve to middle, little line slides to bottom
N	Big line down, frog jump!	Big line slides to bottom, big line goes up
M	Big line down, frog jump!	Big lines slide down, up, and down

2. Copy the capitals on the double lines below the models. Use the same words for the formation directions.
3. Teach children to play the Mystery Letter game with Frog Jump Capitals.
   Wait for all students to put pencils on the dot.
   Say, "Make a starting line down, then frog jump back to the top."
   Then say, "Now make ___." Choose a letter: **F E D P B R N M.**

Tips
- Encourage students to say the directions out loud. Children like to say "ribbit" for the frog jump.
- Notice that when the starting line is on the left edge of the slate, the next part of the letter must be placed on the right side. No reversals!

Get Started Say, "Turn to page 10. These are the Starting Corner Capitals." Demonstrate each letter.

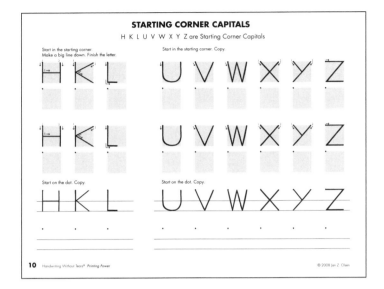

Multisensory Activities

Music and Movement
Use the *Rock, Rap, Tap & Learn* CD. Stand up and slide down to the alphabet for letters **V W X Y Z** with *Sliding Down to the End of the Alphabet,* Track 15. See page 23 of this guide.

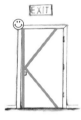

Door Tracing
Prepare your door with the smiley face in the upper left corner. Have children reach for the starting corner and arm trace letters. See page 26 of this guide.

Teach Letters Step-by-Step
1. Copy the capitals in the Gray Blocks below the models. Begin on the dot.
   Follow the directions below for each letter.
   Three capitals begin in the starting corner, with a starting line down.
   - H   Big line down, big line down, little line across (Lefties may make the little line for H like this ←, from right to left.)
   - K   Big line down. Lift pencil to top right corner, kick to middle! Slide away
   - L   Big line down, little line across (Do not pick up the pencil)
2. Look! The six capitals at the end of the alphabet all start in the starting corner.
   - U   Down, travel, and up
   - V   Big line slides down and up
   - W   Big line slides down and up, down and up
   - X   Big line slides down, big line slides down
   - Y   Little line slides down to middle, big line slides down
   - Z   Across, big line slides down, across
3. Copy the capitals on the double lines below the models.
   Use the same words for the formation directions.

Tip
- Choose—If you prefer to use an alternate style for **Y** (**Y**), that's fine. HWT prefers **Y** because it uses the same strokes for both the capital and lowercase letter.

Teach Center Starting Capitals C O Q G S A I T J

Get Started Say, "Turn to page 11. These are the Center Starting Capitals. Watch me. This is capital **C**. I make it like this (demonstrate)." Repeat and demonstrate each letter.

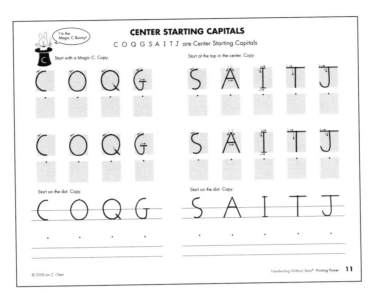

Multisensory Activities

Door Tracing
Prepare your door with the smiley face in the upper left corner. Have children reach for the top center and arm trace letters. To get **C O Q G** started correctly, tell students to go over and say "hello" to the smiley face. See page 26 of this guide.

Mystery Letter on the Slate
Play the Mystery Letter game on the HWT Slate. See page 32 of this guide.

Teach Letters Step-by-Step

1. Copy the capitals in the Gray Blocks below the models.
   Begin on the dot. Follow the directions below for each letter.
   Nine capitals begin at the top center.
   Letters **C O Q G** begin with a Magic C.

C	Make a Magic C.
O	Make a Magic C. Keep on going around. Stop at the top.
Q	Make a Magic C. Keep on going around. Stop at the top. Add a little line.
G	Make a Magic C. Go up. Add a little line.
S	Make a little curve (little Magic c). Turn. Make another little curve.
A	Make a big line slide down, big line slide down, little line across.*
I	Make a big line down, little line across top, little line across bottom.*
T	Make a big line down, little line across top.*
J	Make a big line down, turn, stop; little line across top.*

2. Copy the capitals on the double lines below the models. Use the same words for trhe directions.

   *Lefties may cross this way ←.

Tip
- One side of the Slate has the words Handwriting Without Tears® at the top center. Use this side to help children find the center.

You have taught and reviewed all the capital letters in letter groups. Here is the whole alphabet in alphabetical order for your students to write on double lines.

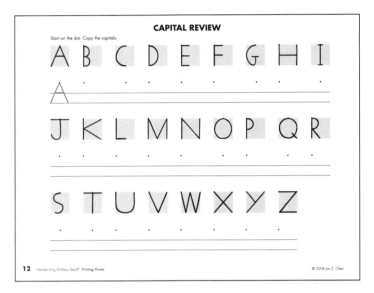

Tell them...

These are all the capitals in alphabetical order. You can see them on the Gray Blocks. You will copy them on double lines. Remember that all capitals start at the top. There is a dot for each letter. That's where you start.

How do I teach this?

Explain how to copy the capitals in ABC order.

Say   Look at the capital **A** in the Gray Block.
Look at the capital **A** on the double lines.
Now look at **B** in the Gray Block.
Copy **B** below **B**. Start on the dot.
Continue copying the whole alphabet.
Start every capital on the dot.

–Supervise while children finish the page.

Review capital formation as needed.

Activity Page – NUMBER PRACTICE

Numbers are taught at the back of the workbook, and you should use those pages during your math instructional time. This page is presented right away for a quick review of correct start, steps, and placement of numbers.

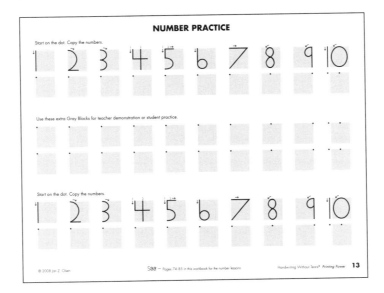

Tell them...
This is a page for writing the numbers **1** to **10** on Gray Blocks. Just like capitals, the numbers start at the top. Numbers **1**, **2**, **3**, **4**, **5**, **6**, and **7** all start in the starting corner. Number **8** starts at the top center. Number **9** has a corner of its own. Number **10** is made with a one that starts on the dot and a zero that starts at the top center.

How do I teach this?

Explain how to copy the numbers in the Gray Blocks.

Say   Look at the top of the page to see the numbers in the Gray Blocks.
           Start on the dot. Copy every number below the model.

–Supervise while children copy
Repeat this activity later at the bottom of the page.

Use the middle section (blank Gray Blocks)
For teacher demonstration (one on one lesson in workbook)

Say   Watch me write number **1**. I start on the dot in the starting corner.
–Wait for student to imitate your **1**.
Say   Watch me write number **2**. I start on the dot in the starting corner.
–Wait for student to imitate your **2**.
Continue   teacher demonstration and student imitation for each number.

For student practice (group activity)

Say   The Gray Blocks in the middle do not have numbers to copy.
           They do have dots to show you where to start.
           Write the numbers **1 2 3 4 5 6 7 8 9 10** in the Gray Blocks.

–Supervise while children write the numbers.
Repeat this activity on the next line.

Tips
• Use pages 74-85 in *Printing Power* for number instruction during math class.

LOWERCASE

Capital Partners

Get Started Say, "Turn to page 14. This is capital **C** and lowercase **c**. Watch me write them. I make them like this." Demonstrate each pair. Use the same step-by-step instructions for the capitals and lowercase.

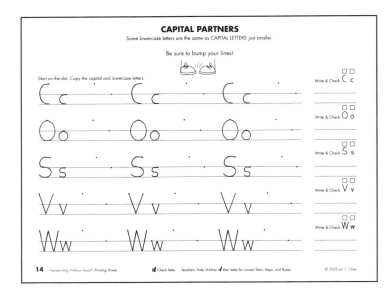

Multisensory Activities

Music and Movement
Use the *Rock, Rap, Tap & Learn* CD. *CAPITALS & lowercase*, Track 16. Have children sing and copy as you model capital **C** and lowercase **c** on the board. You may combine this song with Letter Size and Place.

Letter Size and Place
Demonstrate a capital **C** and lowercase **c**. Hold up hands with the capital first. Repeat for **Oo**, **Ss**, **Vv**, **Ww**. See page 30 of this guide.

Copy and Check Cc, Oo, Ss, Vv, Ww

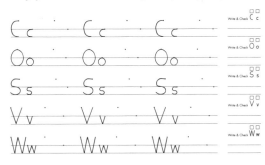

Demonstrate **Cc**.
Children watch, then copy **Cc**s.
☑ Check letters: start, steps, bump
Repeat with other letters.

Tips
- If **c** is too skinny, start on the dot and then travel on the top line before curving down.
- This is the first page in the workbook where we do ☑ Check letter. Teach the concept and components thoroughly. See page 52 of this guide for more information.
- Emphasize tall and small size.
- Teach left-handed students to copy from the model on the right.
- Check Your Teaching, page 117 of this guide.

Teach

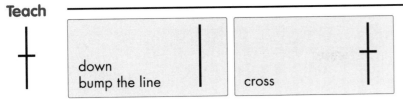

| down bump the line | cross |

Get Started Say, "Turn to page 15. This is lowercase †. Watch me write lowercase †. I make it like this (demonstrate)."

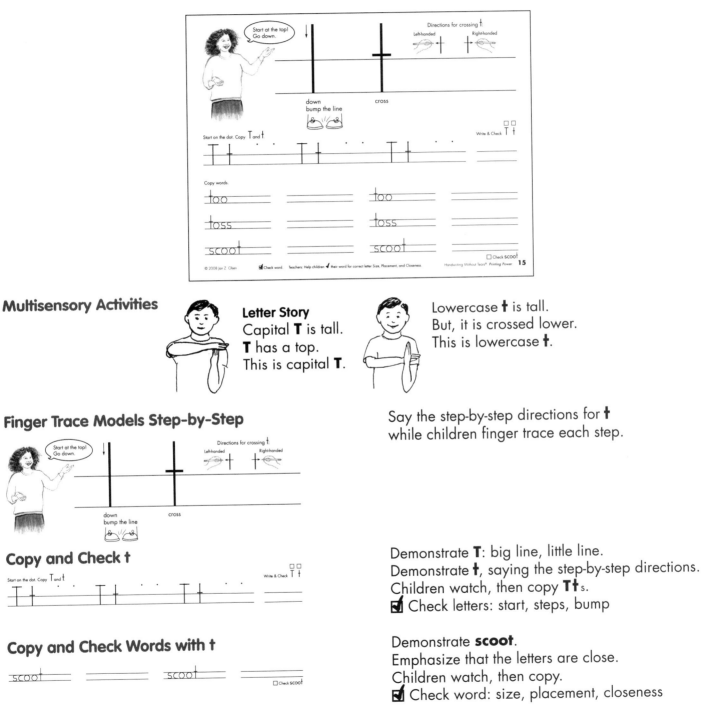

Multisensory Activities

Letter Story
Capital **T** is tall.
T has a top.
This is capital **T**.

Lowercase **†** is tall.
But, it is crossed lower.
This is lowercase **†**.

Finger Trace Models Step-by-Step

Say the step-by-step directions for **†** while children finger trace each step.

Copy and Check t

Demonstrate **T**: big line, little line.
Demonstrate **†**, saying the step-by-step directions.
Children watch, then copy T†s.
☑ Check letters: start, steps, bump

Copy and Check Words with t

Demonstrate **scoot**.
Emphasize that the letters are close.
Children watch, then copy.
☑ Check word: size, placement, closeness

Tips

• This is the first page in the workbook where we do ☑ Check word. Teach the concept and components thoroughly. See page 52 of this guide for more information.
• Students cross **Tt** according to their handedness.
• Mark arrows → for right-handed students. Mark arrows ← for left-handed students.

Multisensory Activity – MAGIC C BUNNY

The Magic C Bunny helps you teach **c**-based lowercase letters **a d g o q**. The Magic C Bunny puppet will bring your lessons to life.

What does the Magic C Bunny do?
- He changes letter **c** into new letters. That's the magic trick.
- He plays Mystery Letter and Voice games.
- He makes learning fun.
- He creates a good Magic c habit for **a d g o** and even **q**.

Multisensory Activities
Music and Movement
Have fun with the *Magic C Rap*, Track 17. This song is a great way to get your students engaged and excited about Magic c letters.
- Introduce Magic **c** while playing the *Magic C Rap*.
- Teach children to sing the chorus:

  Magic c, c for a d and g
  Magic c, c for a d and g
  Magic c, c for a d and g
  And before you're through do o and q

- Introduce the song before demonstrating Magic c letters on the board. Use the Voices activity and have Magic C Bunny whisper which voices your class should use into your ear.

Make the Magic C Bunny

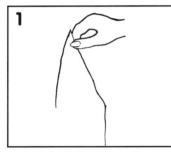

1 Open paper napkin. Hold by one corner.

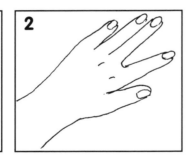

2 Spread index and middle fingers apart.

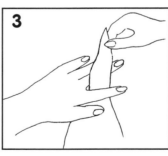

3 Pull corner between your index and middle fingers. (First ear)

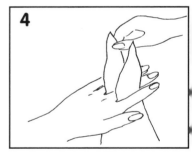

4 Take the next corner. Pull corner between your middle and ring fingers. (Second ear)

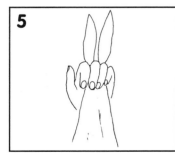

5 Fold fingers into palm.

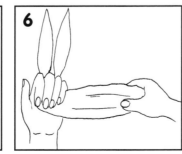

6 Pull napkin out to side.

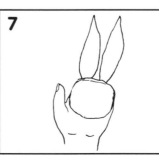

7 Wrap napkin over fingers and tuck into hand.

8 Add the face with a pen. It's a bunny! You may slip the bunny off your fingers and give it to a child. Tape or staple the napkin to hold it.

Teach

| a | Magic c | C | up like a helicopter | C | bump | D | back down bump | a |

Get Started   Say, "Turn to page 16. This is lowercase **a**. Watch me write lowercase **a**. I make it like this (demonstrate)."

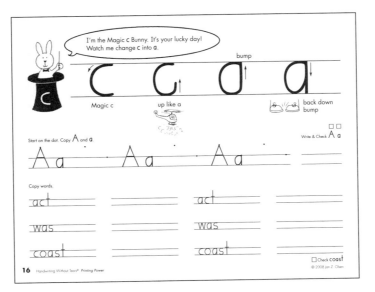

Multisensory Activities

Music and Movement
Use the *Rock, Rap, Tap & Learn* CD. *Magic C Rap*, Track 17. See page 62 of this guide.

Voices
Demonstrate **a** on the board using the Voices activity. See page 31 of this guide.

Finger Trace Models Step-by-Step

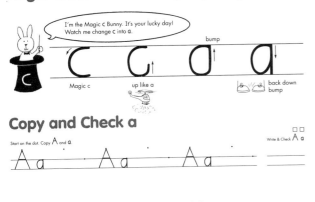

Say the step-by-step directions for **a** while children finger trace each step.

Copy and Check a

Demonstrate **A**: big line, big line, little line.
Demonstrate **a**, saying the step-by-step directions.
Children watch, then copy **Aa**s.
☑ Check letters: start, steps, bump

Copy and Check Words with a

coast   coast

Demonstrate **coast**.
Emphasize that the letters are close.
Children watch, then copy.
☑ Check word: size, placement, closeness

Tips
- If **a** is too skinny, start on the dot and travel on the top line before curving down.
- After students learn **d** and **g**, play the Mystery Letter game on the Blackboard with Double Lines, see page 33 of this guide.

d	Magic c	**C**	up like a helicopter

C	up higher	**d**	back down bump	**d**

Get Started Say, "Turn to page 17. This is lowercase **d**. Watch me write lowercase **d**. I make it like this (demonstrate)."

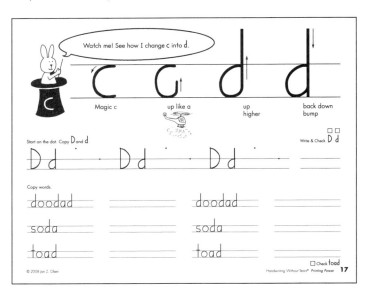

Multisensory Activities

Music and Movement
Use the *Rock, Rap, Tap & Learn* CD, *Magic C Rap*, Track 17. See page 62 of this guide.

Letter Size and Place
Review **a** as a small letter and demonstrate **d** as a tall letter.

a   **d**

Finger Trace Models Step-by-Step

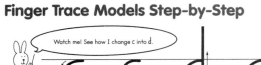

Say the step-by-step directions for **d** while children finger trace each step.

Copy and Check d

Demonstrate **D**: big line, big curve.
Demonstrate **d**, saying the step-by-step directions.
Children watch, then copy **Dd**s.
☑ Check letters: start, steps, bump

Copy and Check Words with d

Demonstrate **toad**.
Emphasize that the letters are close.
Children watch, then copy.
☑ Check word: size, placement, closeness

Tips
• If **d** is short, go up higher like a helicopter.
• If a child doesn't retrace the line down, tell the child to think of sliding down a pole. "Hang on until your feet touch the ground."

Teach

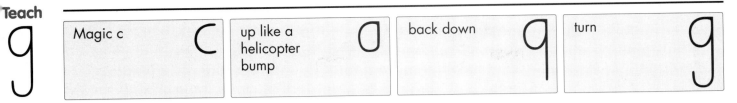

| | Magic c | C | up like a helicopter bump | | back down | | turn | |

Get Started Say, "Turn to page 18. This is lowercase **g**. Watch me write lowercase **g**. I make it like this (demonstrate)."

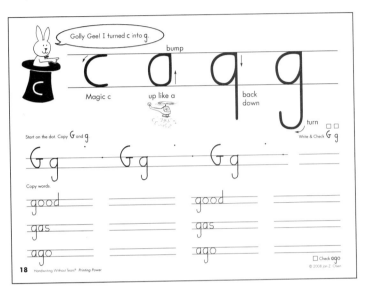

Multisensory Activities

Music and Movement
Use the *Rock, Rap, Tap & Learn* CD, Track 19. Have children sing the chorus of the *Descending Letters*. See page 23 of this guide.

Letter Size and Place
Demonstrate a capital **G** and lowercase **g**. Hold up hands with the capital first.

Letter Story
See page 34 of this guide.

Say the step-by-step directions for **g** while children finger trace each step.

Finger Trace Models Step-by-Step

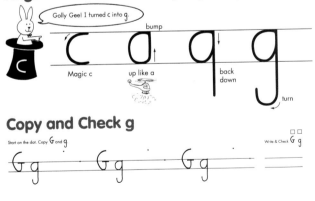

Copy and Check g

Start on the dot. Copy G and g

Demonstrate **G**: big curve, little line, little line.
Demonstrate **g**, saying the step-by-step directions.
Children watch, then copy **Gg**s.
☑ Check letters: start, steps, bump

Copy and Check Words with g

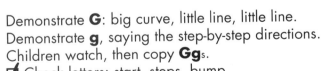

Demonstrate **ago**.
Emphasize that the letters are close.
Children watch, then copy.
☑ Check word: size, placement, closeness

Tips

- If **g** is floating, use the Magic c Silly Spelling activity on page 19 of the workbook.
- If spacing is a problem when writing words, teach students to put letters in a word close to each other. Have them put their index fingers up and bring them close together without touching. Tell them, "In a word, the letters are close, but don't touch." Draw fingers for them.
- Check Your Teaching, page 117 of this guide.

Activity Page – MAGIC C SILLY SPELLING

Want magic? Just have your children make a Magic **c** before they write **o a d** or **g**. Do not name the letter they're making until they trace the **c**. This works magically to ensure that they start **o a d** or **g** correctly.

MAGIC c SILLY SPELLING WORDS
Wait for your teacher to spell the words.

You can make words with Magic C.
Trace C and wait for your teacher.

© 2008 Jan Z. Olsen   See – Teacher's Guide page 66   Handwriting Without Tears® *Printing Power* **19**

Tell them...
Look at all those Magic **c**s. We are going to use them for silly spelling words.

How do I teach this?

Remind them		How to turn **c c c c** into **a d g o**
	Write	**c c c c** on double lines
	Trace	Each **c**. Turn each **c** into a new letter: **a d g o**
Show how to turn		**c c** into **d o**
	Write	**c c**
	Trace	First **c**. Turn it into **d**. Trace the next **c**. Turn it into **o** to make **do**.

Do the Magic c Silly Spelling

Say	Your turn now!
	Trace the first **c**. Wait for me. (Keep pencil at end of **c**.) Turn **c** into **g**.
	Trace the next **c**. Wait for me. (Keep pencil at end of **c**.) Turn **c** into **o**.
	You spelled **go**.
Do	Half the page. Finish another day.

Possible Words:

2 letter **c c** words		do, go, ad – nonsense dc, cg, ag, dg, ao, oa, ac, etc.
3 letter **c c** words		age, oar, cow, gas, cap, car, dot, cot, got, cat, oat, act
c c c words		dog, add, ago, dad, coo, odd, gag, goo, cog
4 letter **c c c** words		coat, goat, cool, cook, cage, dock, goal, doom, door, coal, coop, odor

The FINE Print is a play on words with the name of Edith Fine, a contributor to some of the linguistic insights scattered throughout this guide. In "The Fine Print," you'll find content ranging from advanced instruction to tips that are just for fun. Edith Fine is an accomplished author of children's books designed to teach grammar to elementary school students.

The FINE Print   You may copy pages from this book for extra practice if you have purchased a copy for that child. Magic c Silly Spelling is what you need for children who do not form or place **a d g o** correctly.

© 2008 Jan Z. Olsen

Activity Page – SENTENCES – PUNCTUATION

The words and sentences throughout this page use only previously taught letters. With just a few letters, **c o s v w t a d g**, we can teach three basic sentence skills: 1) Start with a capital 2) Space between words 3) End with a period, exclamation point, or question mark.

SENTENCES - PUNCTUATION

Copy punctuation marks.
Periods • _ _ _ _ _   Question marks ? _ ? _ ? _   Exclamation points ! _ ! _ ! _

Copy sentences. Write under each word.

Was Coco sad? Coco was sad.

Ava saw a toad!

Todd saws. I saw wood too.

☐ Check Sentence

20 *Handwriting Without Tears® Printing Power*   ☑ Check sentence: Teachers: Help children ✓ their sentence for correct Capitalization, Word Spacing, and Ending Punctuation.   © 2008 Jan Z. Olsen

---

Tell them...

This page is about SENTENCES and PUNCTUATION. When we are surprised, you can see it on our faces and hear it in our voices. We sound excited. But when we write, we can't do that. We have to use punctuation. To show surprise, we use an exclamation point. To ask a question, we use a question mark.

How do I teach this?
Show how to make periods, question marks, and exclamation points.

At the board:	Write	• ? !	
	Explain	Use a **•** for a statement:	I am your teacher.
		Use a **?** for a question:	Who am I?
		Use an **!** to show surprise or strong emotion.	I have amazing news!
	Say	Fill in the blanks as I make a statement, ask a question, or exclaim.	

Demonstrate how to write the sentence, "Was Coco sad?," on double lines.

1. Start with a capital.
   At the board: Write   **Was**
   Say   Sentences start with a capital. Capital **W** is like lowercase **w**, but it is higher. Start **W** high.

2. Space between words.
   Write   **Coco sad**
   Say   Put space after every word. Notice that Coco has a capital because Coco is a name, a proper noun.

3. End with a period, question mark, or exclamation point.
   Write   **?**
   Say   This is a question. We end a question with a question mark.
   – Wait for children to copy **Was Coco sad?**

Teach the next sentence.
   Explain   The word order changes in this sentence. This is not a question.
   – Supervise while children finish the page.

The FINE Print   Don't forget the *Sentence Song*, Track 7, *Rock, Rap, Tap & Learn* CD.

U | down, travel, up | U | back down | U

Get Started Say, "Turn to page 21. This is lowercase **u**. Watch me write lowercase **u**. I make it like this (demonstrate)."

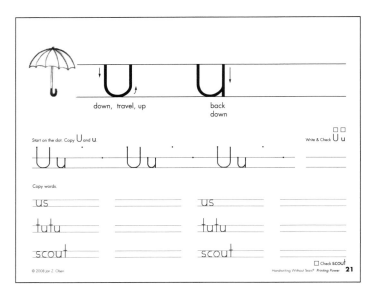

Multisensory Activities

Wet–Dry–Try
Use the Blackboard with Double Lines. See page 24 of this guide.

Imaginary Writing
Follow the Ball and air write **u**. See page 29 of this guide.

Say the step-by-step directions for **u** while children finger trace each step.

Finger Trace Models Step-by-Step

down, travel, up   back down

Copy and Check u

Start on the dot. Copy U and u.   Write & Check U u

Demonstrate **U**: down, travel, and up.
Demonstrate **u**, saying the step-by-step directions.
Children watch, then copy **Uu**s.
☑ Check letters: start, steps, bump

Copy and Check Words with u

scout   scout

Demonstrate **scout**.
Emphasize that the letters are close.
Children watch, then copy.
☑ Check word: size, placement, closeness

Tips
- Teach that **U** and **u** are similar except lowercase **u** has a line.
- If **u** is too pointed like **v**, travel on the bottom line. Take at least two steps on the line and then come straight up.
- Teach careful re-tracing down the line.
- Teach students to put letters in a word close to each other. Have them put their index fingers up and bring them close together, without touching. Tell them, "In a word, the letters are close, but don't touch." Draw fingers for them!

Teach

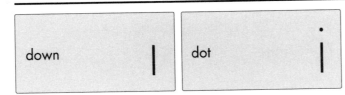

i   down | dot   i

Get Started   Say, "Turn to page 22. This is lowercase **i**. Watch me write lowercase **i**. I make it like this (demonstrate)."

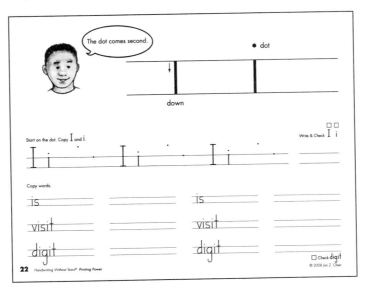

Multisensory Activities

Music and Movement
Use the *Rock, Rap, Tap & Learn* CD, *Vowels*, Track 11.

Wet–Dry–Try
Use the Blackboard with Double Lines. See page 24 of this guide.

Say the step-by-step directions for **i** while children finger trace each step.

Finger Trace Models Step-by-Step

Copy and Check i

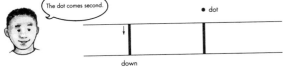

Copy and Check Words with i

Demonstrate **I**: big line, little line, little line.
Demonstrate **i**, saying the step-by-step directions.
Children watch, then copy **I i**s.
☑ Check letters: start, steps, bump

Demonstrate **digit**.
Emphasize that the letters are close.
Children watch, then copy.
☑ Check word: size, placement, closeness

Tips
- Teach the dot.
- Teach children to make the line before the dot. Be flexible about what the dots look like. Allow a little creativity.
- Teach that **I** and **i** are different and **i** is never used alone.

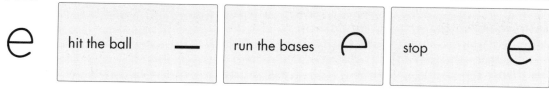

| _e_ | hit the ball | — | run the bases | _e_ | stop | _e_ |

Get Started   Say, "Turn to page 23. This is lowercase **e**. Watch me write lowercase **e**. I make it like this (demonstrate)."

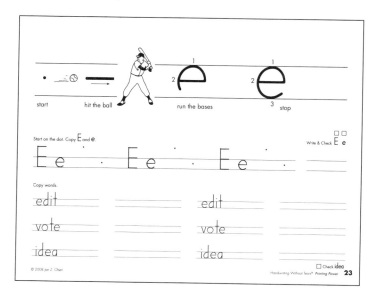

Multisensory Activities

Letter Story
See page 34 of this guide.

Finger Trace Models Step-by-Step

Copy and Check e

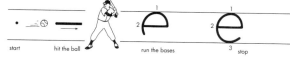

Copy and Check Words with e

idea   idea
☐ Check **idea**

Wet–Dry–Try
Use the Blackboard with Double Lines. See page 24 of this guide.

Say the step-by-step directions for **e** while children finger trace each step.

Demonstrate **E**: big line, little line (3 times).
Demonstrate **e**, saying the step-by-step directions.
Children watch, then copy **Ee**s.
☑ Check letters: start, steps, bump

Demonstrate **idea**.
Emphasize that the letters are close.
Children watch, then copy.
☑ Check word: size, placement, closeness

Tips

- If the beginning of the line isn't straight, practice writing straight dashes between the lines.
- Lowercase **e** does not begin on a line—it begins in the air between the lines. A visual cue (a dot) may be necessary for the child to become comfortable with this concept.
- Remind the child that it is not a home run, "so only run to third base!"
- If spacing is a problem when writing words, teach students to put letters in a word close to each other. Have them put their index fingers up and bring them close together without touching. Tell them, "In a word, the letters are close, but don't touch." Draw fingers for them!

Activity Page – LETTER SIZE AND PLACE

This handy page helps children size and place their letters correctly. The physical motions are fun. See page 30 of this guide for more information about the Letter Size and Place hand activity. This activity should not be used with children learning sign language because it may create confusion.

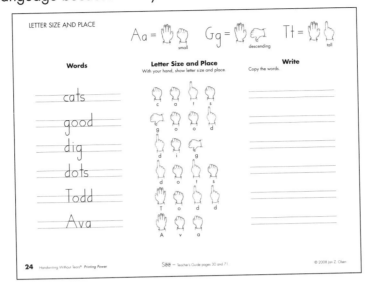

Tell them...
You can use your hands to show letter size. Put both hands flat on the table in front of you. Now hold them up. Change your right hand into a fist. Look at your hands. Your flat hand is the capital **A**. It's tall. Your fisted hand is lowercase **a**. It's small.

How do I teach this?
Do hand motions for c a t s together as a class.
Note: Use a motion as a break between letters. Touch shoulder between letters.

Say	**c**	Make fist
Say	**a**	Make fist
Say	**t**	Point up
Say	**s**	Make fist

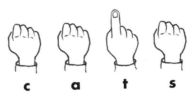

c   a   t   s

Demonstrate writing c a t s on double lines.
At the board: Teach / write **c**   Say **c**   is a small lowercase letter
Teach / write **a**   Say **a**   is a small lowercase letter
Teach / write **t**   Say **t**   is a tall lowercase letter
Teach / write **s**   Say **s**   is a small lowercase letter
– Wait for children to copy **cats**.

Repeat with remaining words.
Do   Hand motions for each word
Teach / write   Words letter by letter
– Wait for children to copy between words

The FINE Print Left-handed children may use the left hand for the this activity.

Activity Page – RHYMING WORDS

Listen! These words rhyme. But the spelling of the rhyme may be different. This page helps second graders notice different spellings for the same sounds. Warn them to use eagle eyes to copy each spelling correctly.

RHYMING WORDS

Read the words out loud.
Listen! They rhyme!

Copy words.

wide - side	save - gave	two - do
scoot - suit	weed - seed	said - wed
tow - go	we - see	toad - sewed

© 2008 Jan Z. Olsen   Handwriting Without Tears® *Printing Power* **25**

Tell them...

Here are more words, and these words rhyme. Rhyming words have the same ending sound. I'll read a few words and you tell me the rhyming sound. **wide – side** _____ **scoot – suit** _____ **tow – go** _____. Look at those words. Sometimes the same ending sound is spelled the same and sometimes it's not.

How do I teach this?
Show them how to write and spell the words.

At the board: Preview   How to write a dash
                    Write / spell   **wide – side**
                    Explain   Same rhyme spelling **-ide**
                — Wait for children to copy.

                    Write / spell   **scoot – suit**
                    Explain   Different rhyme spelling **-oot -uit**
                — Wait for children to copy.

                    Write / spell   **tow – go**
                    Explain   Different rhyme spelling **-ow -o**
                — Wait for children to copy.

                — Supervise while children finish the page.

The FINE Print   Want more? Pick a vowel of the day, perhaps long and short **A**, and use the vowel in rhyming words.
                    List words that end with a long **A** rhyme: play, day, weigh, sleigh, hey.
                    List words with a short **A** rhyme: can, Dan, fan, man, pan, ran, tan, van, at, bat, cat, etc.
                    Find rhyming words alphabetically. Use the Print Wall Cards. Point to consonants as you try each letter as a beginning sound for rhymes. Some will make real words and some will make nonsense words.

Teach

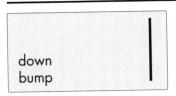

down
bump

Get Started Say, "Turn to page 26. This is lowercase **l**. Watch me write lowercase **l**.
I make it like this (demonstrate)."

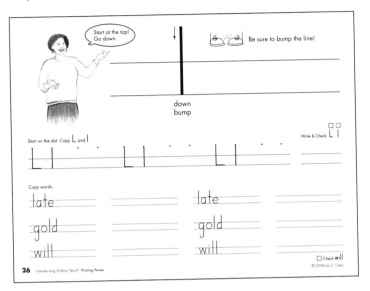

Multisensory Activities

Imaginary Writing
Use *My Teacher Writes* to demonstrate **l**.
See page 28 of this guide.

Finger Trace Models Step-by-Step

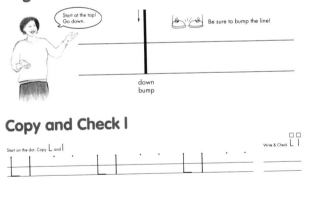

Copy and Check l

Copy and Check Words with l

Letter Size and Place
Teach **L** and **l** are different, but
both begin above the lines.

L   **l**

Say the step-by-step directions for **l**
while children finger trace each step.

Demonstrate **L**: big line, little line.
Demonstrate **l**, saying the step-by-step directions.
Children watch, then copy **Ll**s.
☑ Check letters: start, steps, bump

Demonstrate **will**.
Emphasize that the letters are close.
Children watch, then copy.
☑ Check word: size, placement, closeness

Tip
• If **l** is too short, tell students to begin **l** high above the lines.

Teach

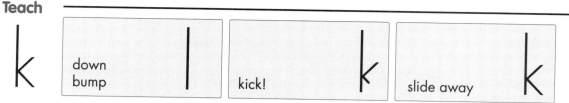

| k | down bump | | kick! | k | slide away | k |

Get Started Say, "Turn to page 27. This is lowercase **k**. Watch me write lowercase **k**. I make it like this (demonstrate)."

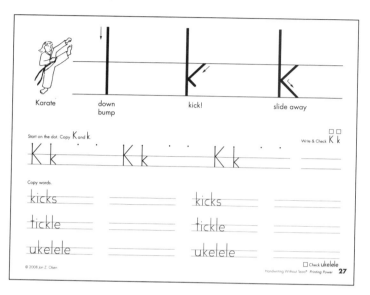

Multisensory Activities

Wet–Dry–Try
Use the Blackboard with Double Lines. See page 24 of this guide.

Mr. Kaye
you

Letter Story
See page 34 of this guide.

Finger Trace Models Step-by-Step

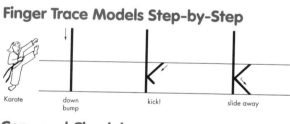

Karate   down bump   kick!   slide away

Say the step-by-step directions for **k** while children finger trace each step.

Copy and Check k

Demonstrate **K**: big line, little line, little line.
Demonstrate **k**, saying the step-by-step directions.
Children watch, then copy **Kk**s.
☑ Check letters: start, steps, bump

Copy and Check Words with k

ukelele   ukelele
☐ Check ukelele

Demonstrate **ukelele**.
Emphasize that the letters are close.
Children watch, then copy.
☑ Check word: size, placement, closeness

Tips

- Encourage the 'hi-yaaaaa' when writing the kick stroke so it's a continuous stroke.
- If spacing is a problem when writing words, teach students to put letters in a word close to each other. Have them put their index fingers up and bring them close together without touching. Tell them, "In a word, the letters are close, but don't touch." Draw fingers for them!

© 2008 Jan Z. Olsen

Activity Page – CAPITALS, COMMAS

Children know about lists: spelling lists, class lists, even grocery lists. There's another way to list items. Write them out in a series. Use commas to separate the items. Here are lists of names, cities, and states. With these lists, students also get capital practice.

CAPITALS, COMMAS

Copy lists.

Names: Ava, Bea, Kate, Sadie, Zoe

Names:

Names: Bill, David, Jose, Mike, Nate

Names:

Cities: Bogota, Osaka, Seoul, Toledo

Cities:

States: Hawaii, Iowa, Alaska, Nevada

States:

28   *Handwriting Without Tears® Printing Power*   © 2008 Jan Z. Olsen

Tell them...
At the top of the page are two words: CAPITALS, COMMAS. One of the words has two meanings. Do you know which one? Capital! There are capital letters and then there are capital cities, cities that are the capitals of countries or states.

How do I teach this?
Introduce capital rules for names.

Say   This page has names. We follow capital rules for names.
             1. Capitalize the names of people.
             2. Capitalize the names of cities.
             3. Capitalize the names of states.
Ask   What else do we capitalize? Months, days, countries, oceans, book titles, etc.

Show one way to write a list.
At the board: Write

Names
Ava
Bea
Kate
Sadie
Zoe

Show another way to write a list.
At the board: Write   **Names:**
                             This is a colon: Use a colon before you start the list
               Write   **Ava, Bea, Kate, Sadie, Zoe**
                             Use a comma after every name, to separate the names.
               — Supervise while children copy the lists.

The FINE Print   These cities and states were chosen because they use only the letters that have been taught. Once you've taught all the letters, have children find and write cities or countries that start with the first letter of their names. More capital and comma practice is as close as your geography book, map, atlas, or globe.

This simple paragraph will make it easy to learn the basics: 1.) Topic 2.) Indenting 3.) Sentences.

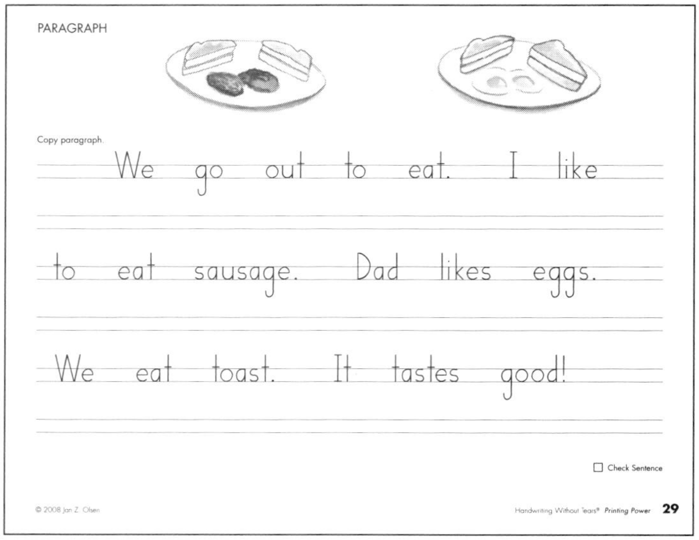

PARAGRAPH

Copy paragraph.

We go out to eat. I like

to eat sausage. Dad likes eggs.

We eat toast. It tastes good!

☐ Check Sentence

© 2008 Jan Z. Olsen   Handwriting Without Tears® *Printing Power* **29**

Tell them...

Even if this page didn't have the word PARAGRAPH on it, we could still tell it's a paragraph page, not a sentence page, or a word or poem page. How can we tell? The first sentence is indented. That's the clue that gives it away.

How do I teach this?

Explain the three paragraph basics.

1. Paragraphs have topics.
> Read   Paragraph aloud and talk about the topic (eating out)

2. Paragraphs are indented.
> At the board: Indent / Write **We go out to eat.**
> — Wait for children to indent and copy.

3. Paragraphs have sentences.
> Explain   Sentences may continue from one line to the next.
> Write   **I like to eat sausage.**
> — Supervise while students finish copying the paragraph.

The FINE Print   Everybody eats! If you're teaching children to write about things in sequence, food can help. Think of making a sandwich, or preparing, serving, and cleaning up after a meal. Special foods for celebrations or holidays are also a good topic.

Teach

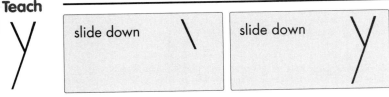

y | slide down | \ | slide down | y

Get Started Say, "Turn to page 30. This is lowercase **y**. Watch me write lowercase **y**.
I make it like this (demonstrate)."

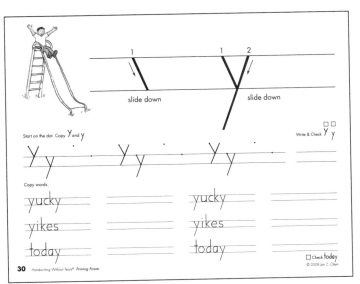

Multisensory Activities

Voices
Demonstrate **y** on the board/
easel using the Voices activity,
page 31 of this guide.

Imaginary Writing
Use a laser and trace letter **y**
on an easel. Children can
follow along in the air. See page
29 of this guide.

Finger Trace Models Step-by-Step

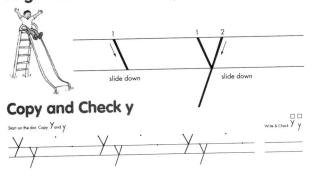

Say the step-by-step directions for **y**
while children finger trace each step.

Copy and Check y

Demonstrate **Y**: little line, big line.
Demonstrate **y**, saying the step-by-step directions.
Children watch, then copy **Yy**s.
☑ Check letters: start, steps, bump

Copy and Check Words with y

Demonstrate **today**.
Emphasize that the letters are close.
Children watch, then copy.
☑ Check word: size, placement, closeness

Tips

- Teach that **Y** and **y** are the same. They're just in different positions.
- Teach that **y** goes below the line.
- You or your student may choose another style for capital **Y** – **Y**.
- If a student slides the stroke the wrong way, count very slowly. One.......Two.............Which comes first?
  One. Make one slide down first. Slide the way the boy in the picture is sliding first.
- Check Your Teaching, page 117 of this guide.

Teach

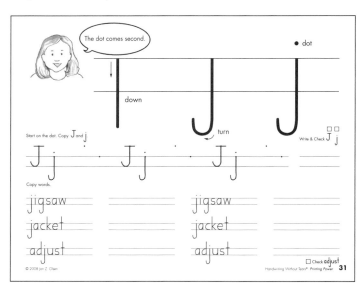

	down	turn	dot
j			

Get Started Say, "Turn to page 31. This is lowercase **j**. Watch me write lowercase **j**. I make it like this (demonstrate)."

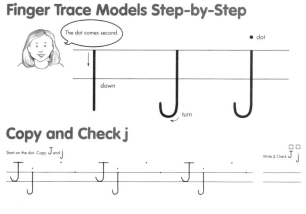

Multisensory Activity

Wet–Dry–Try
Use the Blackboard with Double Lines. See page 24 of this guide.

Finger Trace Models Step-by-Step

Copy and Check j

Copy and Check Words with j

adjust   adjust
☐ Check adjust

Imaginary Writing
Use *My Teacher Writes* to demonstrate **j**. See page 28 of this guide.

Say the step-by-step directions for **j** while children finger trace each step.

Demonstrate **J**: big line, turn, little line.
Demonstrate **j**, saying the step-by-step directions.
Children watch, then copy **Jj**s.
☑ Check letters: start, steps, bump

Demonstrate **adjust**.
Emphasize that the letters are close.
Children watch, then copy.
☑ Check word: size, placement, closeness

Tips

- Teach that **J** and **j** are similar. Point out the differences. They start in different places. They have different tops.
- Teach that **j** goes below the line.
- **J** and **j** turn the same direction as lowercase **g**.
- If **J** and **j** curve too much, make a ruler-straight line down. Turn only at the bottom.

Activity Page – SINGULAR AND PLURAL

Pictures help children understand the words singular and plural. The words on the left side of the page use easy plurals—just add **s**. The words on the right are the tricky ones.

SINGULAR AND PLURAL

Copy words.

tie	ties		goose	geese
suit	suits		kiss	kisses
lake	lakes		sky	skies

32 *Handwriting Without Tears® Printing Power* © 2008 Jan Z. Olsen

---

Tell them...
This page says SINGULAR AND PLURAL. What do you think singular means? Single, or one. Plural means two or more. In English we make most words plural by adding **s**, but not always.

How do I teach this?
Show them how to change singular words into plural words with s.

At the board: Write

tie	**tie**
suit	**suit**
lake	**lake**

Add   **s** to the words on the right.

Explain   **s** makes the words plural.

— Wait for children to copy.

Write   **goose**
            kiss
            sky

Explain   These words do not follow the add **s** rule for making plurals.
            These words make plurals in different ways.

Ask   How do we make plural goose?   Use a different word   **geese**
            How do we make plural kiss?   Add **es**   **kisses**
            How do we make plural sky?   Change **y** to **i**. Add **es**.   **skies**

— Wait for children to copy.

Have children say plural words out loud.

Ask   Students to say the plural word when you say:
            One tiger, two ____, one child, two ____, one dish, two ____, one mouse,
            two ____ etc.

The FINE Print   Here's another fun SINGULAR AND PLURAL activity. Have children work in pairs. Each child makes a list of single items or things in the room. They trade papers and write the plural words.

Activity Page – PARAGRAPH

Children like dogs. Teachers like paragraphs, possessive nouns, and compound words. This page has fun paragraph lessons that appeal to all.

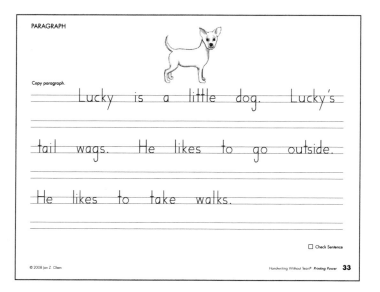

Tell them...

Here's a paragraph about a little dog. Do you know the breed? Chihuahua. Chihuahuas originally came from Mexico. Guess where in Mexico? In Chihuahua, a Mexican state that borders Texas and New Mexico. For a treat, after children finish page 38 of *Printing Power*, teach them the word "Chihuahua." Revisit this page, have them write "Chihuahua" on their paper. You could even make Lucky say, "I am a Chihuahua."

How do I teach this?

Explain the three paragraph basics.

1. Paragraphs have topics.

Read	Paragraph aloud and talk about the topic (Chihuahua)

2. Paragraphs are indented.

At the board: Indent / Write **Lucky is a little dog. Lucky's**
— Wait for children to indent and copy.

3. Paragraphs have sentences.

Explain	Sentences may continue from one line to the next.
Write	**tail wags.**

Show how to use 's to show possession.

At the board	Write	**Lucky's**
	Explain	**'s** means possession. The tail belongs to Lucky.

Explain the compound word – outside.

At the board	Write	**out** + **side** = **outside**
	Explain	Compound words are made from two words.

— Supervise while students finish copying the paragraph.

The FINE Print   Dogs are an ideal paragraph topic. Children may have a favorite dog from a book. Working dogs are interesting too.

Multisensory Activity – DIVER LETTERS

18

Take your students to *Diver Letters' School*, Track 18, and teach them the diver letters. The diver letters are **p r n m h b**. They all start with a diver motion: dive down, swim up, and over.

Diver Letters' School

Boys and girls, welcome to diver school
Stand up and get ready

When you dive in a pool
It makes you feel so cool
When you dive in a pool
It makes you feel so cool

You have to stand up straight, oh yeah (2X)
And you shake, shake, shake, oh yeah (2X)
You put your arms up straight, way up (2X)
And then you WAIT, WAIT, WAIT!
And then you wait, wait, wait...

Are you ready...are you ready?
Here we goooooooooo....
Deep breath

Dive down, swim up and over
What fun!
Dive down, swim up, and over
We're not done!

Dive down, swim up, and over
You better!
Dive down, swim up, and over
In diver letters!

Let's try it faster!
Are you ready?
Here we goooooooooo...
Deep breath

Dive down, swim up, and over
What fun!
Dive down, swim up, and over
We're not done!

Dive down, swim up, and over
You better!
Dive down, swim up, and over
in diver letters!

Tips

- Toss out pretend swimming suits to your class to put on.
- Bring in your own whistle to whistle with the CD.

P | dive down | | swim up and over | | around bump | P

Get Started Say, "Turn to page 34. This is lowercase **p**. Watch me write lowercase **p**. I make it like this (demonstrate)."

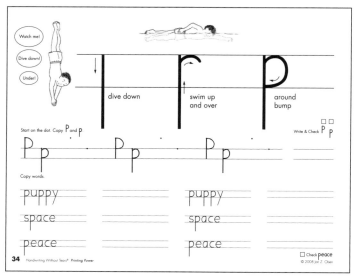

Multisensory Activities

Music and Movement
Use the *Rock, Rap, Tap & Learn* CD, *Diver Letters' School,* Track 18. See page 81 of this guide.

Letter Size and Place
P is tall. Lowercase **p** is descending. See page 30 of this guide.

P   **p**

Finger Trace Models Step-by-Step

Say the step-by-step directions for **p** while children finger trace each step.

Copy and Check p

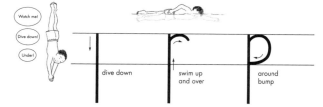

Demonstrate **P**: big line, little curve.
Demonstrate **p**, saying the step-by-step directions.
Children watch, then copy **Pp**s.
☑ Check letters: start, steps, bump

Copy and Check Words with p

Demonstrate **peace**.
Emphasize that the letters are close.
Children watch, then copy.
☑ Check word: size, placement, closeness

Tips
• Capital **P** has been taught with two strokes. Your students may make **P** with a continuous stroke.
• If re-tracing is a problem, tell them they are in a diving competition. They must dive down and come straight up in the bubbles.

r | dive down | l | swim up and over | r

Get Started   Say, "Turn to page 35. This is lowercase **r**. Watch me write lowercase **r**. I make it like this (demonstrate)."

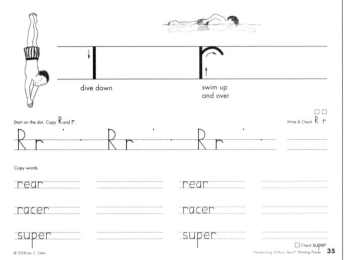

Multisensory Activities

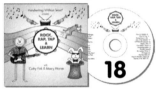

Music and Movement
Use the *Rock, Rap, Tap & Learn* CD, *Diver Letters' School*, Track 18. See page 81 of this guide.

Wet–Dry–Try
Use the Blackboard with Double Lines. See page 24.

Finger Trace Models Step-by-Step

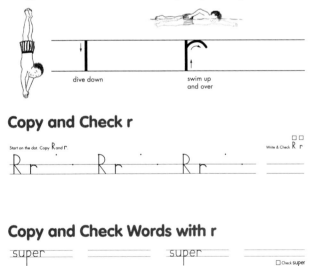

Say the step-by-step directions for **r** while children finger trace each step.

Copy and Check r

Demonstrate **R**: big line, little curve, little line.
Demonstrate **r**, saying the step-by-step directions.
Children watch, then copy **Rr**s.
☑ Check letters: start, steps, bump

Copy and Check Words with r

Demonstrate **super**.
Emphasize that the letters are close.
Children watch, then copy.
☑ Check word: size, placement, closeness

Tips

• Capital **R** has been taught with three strokes. Your students may make **R** with a continuous stroke.
• If re-tracing is a problem, tell them the pencil must retrace until it gets to the top line and can swim over.

n	dive down	l	swim up and over	r	down	n

Get Started Say, "Turn to page 36. This is lowercase **n**. Watch me write lowercase **n**. I make it like this (demonstrate)."

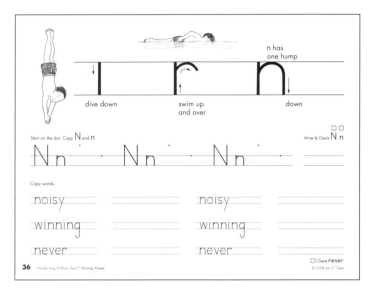

Multisensory Activities

Music and Movement
Use the *Rock, Rap, Tap & Learn* CD, *Diver Letters' School*, Track 18. See page 81 of this guide.

Letter Size and Place
N is tall and **n** is small. Lowercase **n** fits between the lines.

Finger Trace Models Step-by-Step

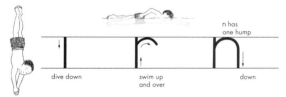

Say the step-by-step directions for **n** while children finger trace each step.

Copy and Check n

Demonstrate **N**: big line, big line, big line.
Demonstrate **n**, saying the step-by-step directions.
Children watch, then copy **Nn**s.
☑ Check letters: start, steps, bump

Copy and Check Words with n

Demonstrate **never**.
Emphasize that the letters are close.
Children watch, then copy.
☑ Check word: size, placement, closeness

Tips
- Be sure the **n** is started on the top line.
- If **n** finishes with a slide, teach that **n** comes straight down. No sliding allowed.
- If re-tracing is a problem, explain that the pencil must retrace until it gets to the top line and can swim over.

Teach

Get Started Say, "Turn to page 37. This is lowercase **m**. Watch me write lowercase **m**.
I make it like this (demonstrate)."

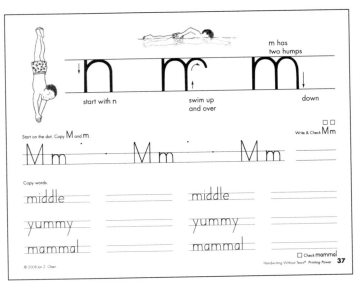

Multisensory Activities

Music and Movement
Use the *Rock, Rap, Tap & Learn* CD,
Diver Letters' School, Track 18.
See page 81 of this guide.

Letter Story
See page 35
of this guide.

Finger Trace Models Step-by-Step

Say the step-by-step directions for **m**
while children finger trace each step.

Copy and Check m

Demonstrate **M**: big line, big line, big line, big line.
Demonstrate **m**, saying the step-by-step directions.
Children watch, then copy **Mm**s.
☑ Check letters: start, steps, bump

Copy and Check Words with m

Demonstrate **mammal**.
Emphasize that the letters are close.
Children watch, then copy.
☑ Check word: size, placement, closeness

Tips
- If re-tracing is a problem, explain that the pencil must retrace until it gets to the top line and can swim over.
- If spacing is a problem when writing words, teach students to put letters in a word close to each other. Have them put their index fingers up and bring them close together without touching. Tell them, "In a word, the letters are close, but don't touch." Draw fingers for them!

h | dive down | | swim up and over | ʰ | down | h

Get Started Say, "Turn to page 38. This is lowercase **h**. Watch me write lowercase **h**. I make it like this (demonstrate)."

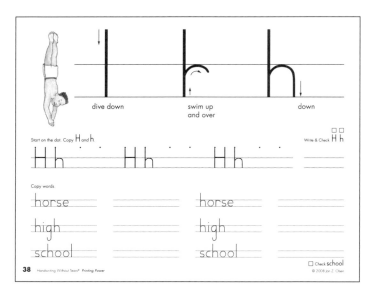

Multisensory Activities

18

Music and Movement
Use the *Rock, Rap, Tap & Learn* CD, *Diver Letters' School*, Track 18. See page 81 of this guide.

Letter Size and Place
H and **h** are both tall.

H   h

Finger Trace Models Step-by-Step

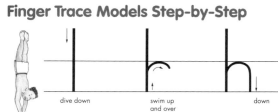

Say the step-by-step directions for **h** while children finger trace each step.

Copy and Check h

Demonstrate **H**: big line, big line, little line.
Demonstrate **h**, saying the step-by-step directions.
Children watch, then copy **Hh**s.
☑ Check letters: start, steps, bump

Copy and Check Words with h

Demonstrate **school**.
Emphasize that the letters are close.
Children watch, then copy.
☑ Check word: size, placement, closeness

Tips
- If **h** is too short, emphasize the **h** as a high dive that starts way up in the air.
- If **h** finishes with a slide, teach that **h** comes straight down. No sliding allowed.
- If retracing is a problem, the pencil must retrace until it gets to the top line and can swim over.

Teach

dive
down

swim up
and over

around
bump

Get Started   Say, "Turn to page 39. This is lowercase **b**. Watch me write lowercase **b**.
I make it like this (demonstrate)."

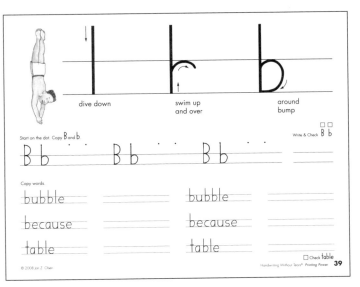

Multisensory Activities

Music and Movement
Use the *Rock, Rap, Tap & Learn* CD,
Diver Letters' School, Track 18.
See page 81 of this guide.

Letter Story
See page 34 of this guide.

Finger Trace Models Step-by-Step

dive down

swim up
and over

around
bump

Say the step-by-step directions for **b**
while children finger trace each step.

Copy and Check b

Demonstrate **B**: big line, little curve, little curve.
Demonstrate **b**, saying the step-by-step directions.
Children watch, then copy **Bb**s.
☑ Check letters: start, steps, bump

Copy and Check Words with b

Demonstrate **table**
Emphasize that the letters are close.
Children watch, then copy.
☑ Check word: size, placement, closeness

Tips

- To help children who come to you with **b** and **d** confusion, teach them **b** by starting with **h** and teach **d** by starting with **c**.
- Check Your Teaching, page 117 of this guide.

Activity Page – TURNING **h** INTO **b**

Goodbye **b/d** confusion! Teach children to think of **h** for honey bee. Turning **h** into **b** ensures that **b** is correct.

TURN h into b

Trace the start. Make letter b.

Copy.

Here is an h for a honey-bee.

Copy the h and b rhymes.

hat - bat   hop - bop   he - be

heat - beat   hug - bug   hall - ball

40   Handwriting Without Tears® *Printing Power*   © 2008 Jan Z. Olsen

Tell them...

I want you to think of letters **h** and **b**. They are very similar. They are both tall letters. They both start at the top. They are diver letters. In fact, they are so much alike that you can start to make an **h** and turn it into a **b**.

How do I teach this?

Have them stand up and do the diver motions. See page 81 of this guide.
Note: Teachers do this facing the class. Teacher should do the swim over motion to the teacher's left so that the motion for the students will be to the right.

Say and move	Get ready for a high dive. Climb the ladder. Start high.
	Dive down, swim up, swim over.

Have them sit to do air letters for **h** and **b**.
Note: Teachers do this facing the class. The teacher's letter should do the swim over motion to the teacher's left so the the letters **h** and **b** will go to the right side for the students. Teachers hold a ball or bright object so that the students can easily point to the object.

Say and move	Point to the ball. Follow it with your finger as it moves.
	Start high.
	Dive down, swim up, swim over and down. That's an **h**.
Repeat with a change	We're going to do that again, and I have a surprise at the end.
	Point to the ball. Follow it with your finger as it moves.
	This time we'll say, "Here is an **h**," as we trace **h** in the air.
At the end say,	Here is an **h** for a honeybee.
	Turn **h** into **b**.

Tell students to copy the sentence, turn the diving strokes into letter **b**s, and copy the words.

Activity Page – WORD SEARCH

Why a word search? It's a perfect opportunity for you to check how well your children are remembering and writing lowercase letters. The activity requires them to change capitals into lowercase.

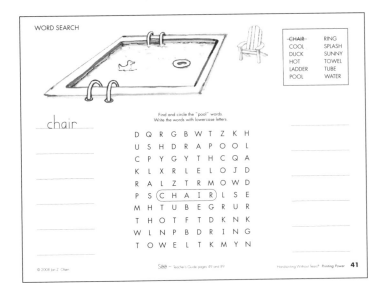

Tell them...
There are words hiding in these letters. Some are horizontal like this → and some are vertical like this ↑↓. There are no diagonal words.

How do I teach this?

Demonstrate   Strategy for finding words horizontally.

Look across each row from left to right searching for words.

Use Row 6 – P S **C H A I R** L S E as an example for searching, circling, and writing

Row 1 – D Q R G B W T Z K H – No word

Row 2 – U S H D R A **P O O L**

Find and circle   **POOL**

Write   **pool** in lowercase under the word chair.

Cross out   **POOL** in the word chart.

Row 3 – C P Y G Y T H C Q A – No word

Row 4 – K L X R L E L O J D – No word

Row 5 – R A L Z T R M O W D – No word (Mow is a word, but not a listed water word)

Row 6 – Example row

Row 7 – M H **T U B** E G R U R   – TUB   –   Find, circle, write, and cross out the word.

Row 8 – **T H O T** F T D K N K   – HOT   –   Find, circle, write, and cross out the word.

Row 9 – W L N P B D **R I N G**   – RING   –   Find, circle, write, and cross out the word.

Row 10 – **T O W E L** T K M Y N – TOWEL –   Find, circle, write, and cross out the word.

Demonstrate   Strategy for finding words vertically.

Look down each column from top to bottom searching for words. Do as above.

Column 1. DUCK   2. SPLASH   3. No word   4. No word   5. WATER

6. No word   7. No word   8. COOL   9. SUN   10. LADDER

up
down

cross

Get Started Say, "Turn to page 42. This is lowercase **f**. Watch me write lowercase **f**. I make it like this (demonstrate)."

Multisensory Activities

Wet–Dry–Try
Use the Blackboard with Double Lines. See page 24 of this guide.

Letter Story
See page 34 of this guide.

Finger Trace Models Step-by-Step

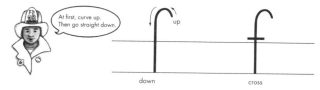

Say the step-by-step directions for **f** while children finger trace each step.

Copy and Check f

Demonstrate **F**: big line, little line, little line.
Demonstrate **f**, saying the step-by-step directions.
Children watch, then copy **Ff**s.
☑ Check letters: start, steps, bump

Copy and Check Words with f

after   after

Demonstrate **after**.
Emphasize that the letters are close.
Children watch, then copy.
☑ Check word: size, placement, closeness

Tip
• If children start **f** with a big line, teach them the letter story.

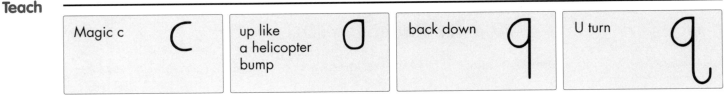

| Magic c | C | up like a helicopter bump | a | back down | q | U turn | q |

Get Started   Say, "Turn to page 43. This is lowercase **q**. Watch me write lowercase **q**. I make it like this (demonstrate)."

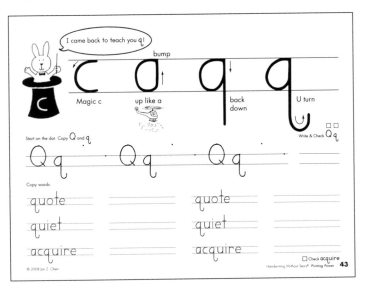

Multisensory Activities

Voices
Demonstrate **q** on the board/easel using the Voices activity, page 31 of this guide.

Letter Story
For children who confuse **g** with **q**, teach the Letter Story. See page 35 of this guide.

Finger Trace Models Step-by-Step

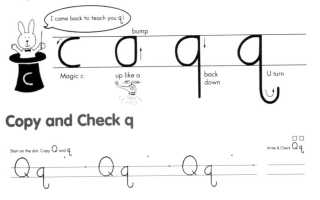

Say the step-by-step directions for **q** while children finger trace each step.

Copy and Check q

Demonstrate **Q**: big curve, big curve, little line.
Demonstrate **q**, saying the step-by-step directions.
Children watch, then copy **Qq**s.
☑ Check letters: start, steps, bump

Copy and Check Words with q

Demonstrate **acquire**.
Emphasize that the letters are close.
Children watch, then copy.
☑ Check word: size, placement, closeness

Tip
- The letter **q** is always followed by **u**. Teach children to finish **q** with a u-turn so they can practice writing the next letter in the word.
- If children reverse **q**, teach them the letter story.

Activity Page – PARAGRAPH

Take your class on a trip to ancient Rome. This is another great way to review paragraph basics.

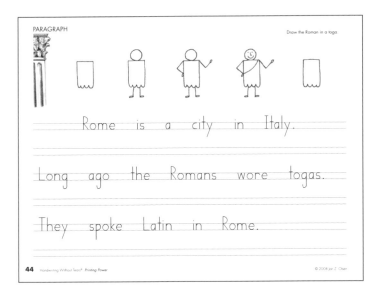

Tell them...

Long, long, ago before zippers and buttons were invented, the men in Rome wore togas. Rome is a city in Italy. This is a paragraph about Rome.

How do I teach this?

Show how to draw a step-by-step picture.

At the board:	Draw	Starting toga shape.
	Draw	Each part in order for children to copy.
	— Wait for children to draw each step.	

Review the three paragraph basics.

1. Paragraphs have a topic.

	Read	Paragraph aloud together.
	Ask	What is the topic? (Rome and Romans)

2. Paragraphs are indented.

	Explain	We indent the first sentence in a paragraph.
		To indent, we move over a big space BEFORE we write.
At the board:	Indent / Write	**Rome is a city in Italy.**
	Explain	**Italy.** We capitalize the names of countries.
	— Wait for children to indent and copy.	

3. Paragraphs have sentences.

	Explain	Each sentence takes only one line in this example.
At the board:	Write	**Long ago Romans wore togas.**
	Write	**They spoke Latin in Rome.**
		Latin. Latin is a language. We capitalize the names of languages.
	— Supervise while children finish copying the paragraph.	

The FINE Print   These two pages can come to life. Sheets can be togas. Paper tubes can be columns. Be sure to locate Rome on a map.

Activity Page – LATIN GREEK

Keep your toga on! It's time for some Latin and Greek. Tricycle and submarine are familiar, but microscope might be new. Knowing the meaning of prefixes—micro, tri, sub; and roots: scope, cycle, mar—helps children figure out big, long words.

LATIN GREEK

microscope	tricycle	submarine
micro : small	tri : three	sub : under
scope : look at	cycle : wheel	mar : sea
microscope	tricycle	submarine

© 2008 Jan Z. Olsen   Handwriting Without Tears® *Printing Power* **45**

Tell them...
See LATIN GREEK on top of the column. Latin and Greek are languages. When we use words like **microscope**, **tricycle**, or **submarine**, we are using Latin or Greek words. English is a language that uses words from other languages.

How do I teach this?
Explain prefixes:
At the board: Write   **micro, tri, sub = prefixes**
                     microscope tricycle submarine

           Explain   Prefixes come at the beginning of words. I'll underline them.
                     micro, tri, and **sub** are Latin or Greek words.
                     Let's read what they mean: **micro = small, tri = three, sub = under**
    — Wait while students underline the prefixes in words: <u>micro</u>scope, <u>tri</u>cycle, <u>sub</u>marine.
    — Wait while students copy the prefixes and their meanings.

Explain word roots:
At the board: Write   **scope**   **cycle**   **mar = roots**
           Circle   **micro(scope)**   **tri(cycle)**   **sub(mar)ine**
           Explain   Roots are the main parts of words.
                     Let's read what they mean: **scope = look at, cycle = wheel, mar = sea**
    — Wait while students circle the roots: <u>micro</u> (scope), <u>tri</u> (cycle), <u>sub</u> (mar) ine
    — Wait while students copy the roots and their meanings.

The FINE Print   Keep going! Look at that submarine. It has a periscope, peri = around. Don't forget unicycles and bicycles; uni = one, bi = two. *Crytomania*, by Edith H. Fine, is a book that transports kids to a world of Latin and Greek.

Teach

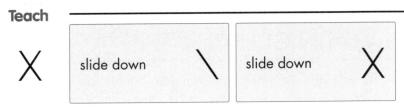

X   slide down   \   slide down   X

Get Started   Say, "Turn to page 46. This is lowercase **x**. Watch me write lowercase **x**. I make it like this (demonstrate)."

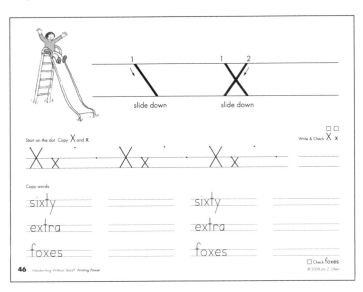

Multisensory Activities

Music and Movement
Use the *Rock, Rap, Tap & Learn* CD. Have children sing *Diagonals*, Track 5.

Imaginary Writing
Use *Air Writing* to demonstrate **x**. See page 28 of this guide.

Finger Trace Models Step-by-Step

Say the step-by-step directions for **x** while children finger trace each step.

Copy and Check x

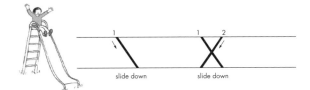

Demonstrate **X**: big line, big line.
Demonstrate **x**, saying the step-by-step directions.
Children watch, then copy **Xx**s.
☑ Check letters: start, steps, bump

Copy and Check Words with x

Demonstrate **foxes**.
Emphasize that the letters are close.
Children watch, then copy.
☑ Check word: size, placement, closeness

Tip

• If diagonal lines are a problem, have children finger trace the slide illustration on their page.

Teach

| Z | go across | — | slide down | 7 | go across | Z |

Get Started   Say, "Turn to page 47. This is lowercase **z**. Watch me write lowercase **z**.
I make it like this (demonstrate)."

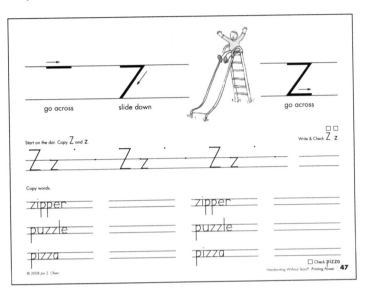

Multisensory Activity

Music and Movement
Use the *Rock, Rap, Tap & Learn* CD,
Sliding Down to the End of the Alphabet, Track 15.
Stand up and slide down to the end of the alphabet
for letters **V W X Y Z**.

Finger Trace Models Step-by-Step

go across   slide down   go across

Say the step-by-step directions for **z**
while children finger trace each step.

Copy and Check z

Start on the dot. Copy Z and z.   Write & Check Z z

Demonstrate **Z**: little line, big line, little line.
Demonstrate **z**, saying the step-by-step directions.
Children watch, then copy **Zz**s.
☑ Check letters: start, steps, bump

Copy and Check Words with z

pizza   pizza   ☐ Check pizza

Demonstrate **pizza**.
Emphasize that the letters are close.
Children watch, then copy.
☑ Check word: size, placement, closeness

Tip
• Check Your Teaching, page 117 of this guide.

This lowercase letter review will challenge memory orientation, and placement skills.

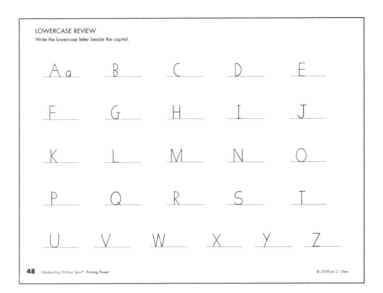

Tell them...

This is a page for reviewing all the lowercase letters in alphabetical order. Some lowercase letters are as tall as capitals, some are small, and a few are descending. You will write the lowercase letter for each capital letter.

How do I teach this?

Explain how to write the lowercase letters in alphabetical order beside the capitals.
Say   Look at the capital **A** on the line.
         Look at the small lowercase **a** beside the capital **A**.
         Now look at the next letter, **B**.
Write the lowercase **b** beside **B**.
Ask   Is **b** a small or tall lowercase letter? It's tall. Make lowercase **b** as tall as capital **B**.
— Wait for students to write **b**.
Say   Now continue writing the other lowercase letters. Think about whether the lowercase letter is as tall as the capital, is smaller than the capital, or descends below the line.
— Supervise while children finish the page.
Review lowercase letters as needed.

Activity Page – LETTER – SENTENCE FUN

Handwriting instruction progresses in three stages: imitation, copying, and independent writing.
Fun Sentences are independent writing.

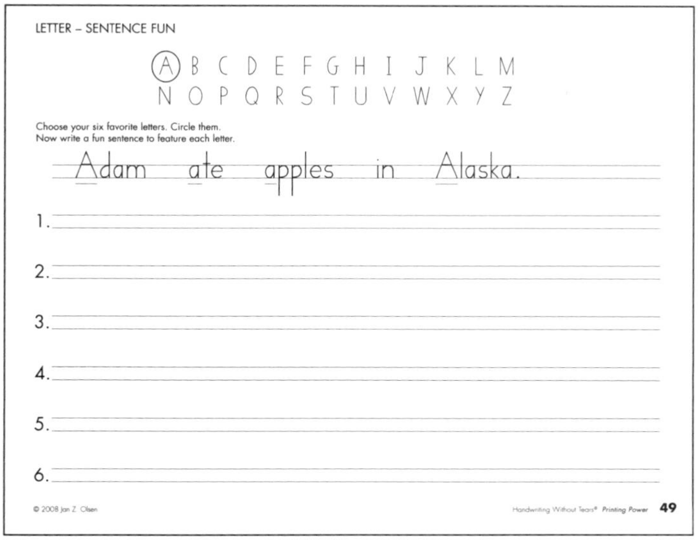

LETTER – SENTENCE FUN

Ⓐ B C D E F G H I J K L M
N O P Q R S T U V W X Y Z

Choose your six favorite letters. Circle them.
Now write a fun sentence to feature each letter.

Adam ate apples in Alaska.

1. _____
2. _____
3. _____
4. _____
5. _____
6. _____

© 2008 Jan Z. Olsen   Handwriting Without Tears® *Printing Power* **49**

Tell them...

You have favorite letters. Maybe you like to write them, maybe you like their shape, maybe they're letters that start your name. On this page, you are going to have fun with your favorite letters.

How do I teach this?

		Subject	Verb	Object	Preposition	Object
	Explain	Each sentence must feature a single letter. Silly sentences are fine!				
At the board:	Write	Form and fill in the sample sentence.				
	Write	Adam	ate	apples	from	Alaska.
	Write	Barbara	bought	books	in	Boston.
	Ask	Students to help you compose a fun letter sentence for letters **C** and **D**.				

— Supervise students as they make up their own sentences.

The FINE Print   If you'd like your students to use a variety of prepositions, write a few prepositions on the board for them.

to	with	under	over	behind

Teaching nothing (spaces) is as important as teaching letters. When letters are close, we can see that it's a word. When spaces separate words we can see individual words easily. It's spacing that makes printing easy to read.

SENTENCE SPACING
Copy the tips about letter and word spacing.

Put letters in words close.

Put space after words.

Help! The question needs to be fixed. Rewrite the question using correct spacing.

A r e t h e l e t t e r s c l o s e ?

☐ Check Sentence

50   Handwriting Without Tears® *Printing Power*   © 2008 Jan Z. Olsen

SENTENCE SPACING
Copy the tips about letter and word spacing.

Don't forget the spaces.

Put space after words.

Help! The question needs to be fixed. Rewrite the question using correct spacing.

How are the spaces?

☐ Check Sentence

© 2008 Jan Z. Olsen   Handwriting Without Tears® *Printing Power*   51

Tell them...
Look at the bottom of page 50. That question is hard to read because the letters in the words are not close, and there are not spaces between the words. The tips are easy to read. They use good spacing.

How do I teach this?
Teach that letters in words are close.

Demonstrate	Put your index fingers horizontal, pointing to each other. Put them as close as you can, without touching. That's close.
Say	When you write letters in a word, put them that close. Now copy the sentence: Put letters in words close.

Teach that space comes after words.

Demonstrate	Pretend to pour nothing out of a big empty bottle into your children's cupped hand.
Say	I gave you nothing. Nothing helps us see the words. Now copy the sentence: Put space after words.

Teach how to correct a poorly written sentence.

Say	The question at the bottom is hard to read. You can make it easy to read if you rewrite it. Do not copy below the letters. Rewrite it correctly. Put the letters, **A - r - e**, close together to write **Are**. Leave a space after **Are**.
Ask	What is the next word? (the)
Say	Put the letters, **t – h – e**, close together to write **the**. Leave a space after **the**.

Tell them...
Look at page 51. The tips are easy to read, but the question is hard to read. Can you tell me why?

Teach that space comes after words.

Say	The tips on this page are about spaces. Copy the tips.

Teach how to correct a poorly written sentence.

Say	The question at the bottom is hard to read. It is hard to read because there are no spaces after the words. You can make it easy to read. Do not copy below. Rewrite this question with spaces after every word.
—	Supervise while students rewrite the question the way it should be written.

Activity Page – PARAGRAPH

Perhaps you or a student in your class knows American Sign Language and can share some signs with the class.

PARAGRAPH

A B C D E F G H I J K L M

N O P Q R S T U V W X Y Z **PAINT**

Some people use sign language.

Pretend to paint your hand with your

fingers. That is the sign for "paint."

52 *Handwriting Without Tears® Printing Power*   © 2008 Jan Z. Olsen

Tell them...
This paragraph is about sign language. Sign language uses finger spelling to spell names and certain words. But signs are faster and they don't need letters. Some signs, like paint or break, are easy to remember because they use a familiar motion or gesture.

How do I teach this?
Review the three paragraph basics.
1 Paragraphs have topics.

       Read   Paragraph aloud together.

       Ask   What is the topic? (sign language)

2. Paragraphs are indented.

    At the board: Indent / Write **Some people use sign language.**

3. Paragraphs have sentences.

       Ask   Is that the end of the sentence? Yes.

       Explain   Some sentences take more then one line.

    — Supervise while students copy the paragraph.

Activity Page – POEM

Do your students know any poems or nursery rhymes? Here's a poem that's more fun than your ordinary contraction lesson. You can teach apostrophes, contractions, and poetry on one fun page.

POEM

Apostrophe

I can spell doesn't and don't

I can spell wasn't and won't

But please, please, don't ask me

To spell apostrophe.

© 2008 Jan Z. Olsen   Handwriting Without Tears® *Printing Power* **53**

Tell them...

The title of this poem is *Apostrophe*. Apostrophe is a very big word (10 letters) for a very little mark. (Show them.) Apostrophes have two uses. One is for showing ownership or possession: Zoe's dog, Harry's house, etc. The other use is for making contractions. Let's read the poem together and see if you can find the contractions.

How do I teach this?

Explain the basics as they copy the poem.

1. Poems have titles.

Read	*Apostrophe* and the poem aloud together.
Explain	Poems have titles. The people who write the poems write the titles.

2. Poems have lines.

At the board:

Write	**I can spell doesn't and don't**
Explain	This is a line. Lines start with capitals.

— Wait for children to copy.

Write	**I can spell wasn't and won't**
Explain	This is the next line. Lines start with capitals.

— Wait for children to copy.

3. Poems use rhyme. (They also have rhythm or meter, but do that another day!)

At the board:

Write	**But please, please, don't ask me**
Explain	This is a line. Lines start with capitals.

— Wait for children to copy.

Write	**To spell apostrophe.**
Explain	This is the last line. Let's read the last words of each line: don't, won't, me, apostrophe. They rhyme. They have the same ending sound, **on't**, and long **E**.

— Wait for children to copy.

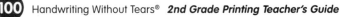

Activity Page – QUOTATIONS

Get out the comics and funny papers! The easiest way to understand and teach quotations is with bubble quotes. Quotations are a person's exact words, directly from a person's mouth. Seeing the bubbles helps children understand this concept.

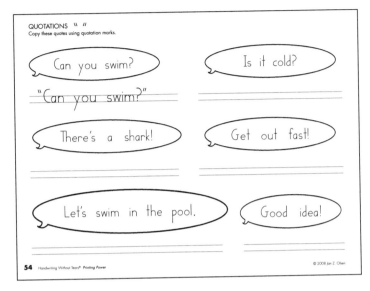

Tell them...
You have seen these quote bubbles before! They are used in comic books and funny papers. I want you to look at the end of the bubbles. See the punctuation. The quotes end with a question mark, exclamation point, or period.

How do I teach this?
Quote bubbles and quotation marks show a person's exact words.

At the board:	Ask	What are the bubbles for? They are for a person's exact words—straight from the mouth.
	Write	" "
	Explain	These are quotation marks. They hold the quote, the exact words.

Show how to change the bubble quote into "Can you swim?"

At the board:	Write	**"Can you swim?"**
		— Wait for children to copy.
	Say	Now change the other bubble quotes into quotations. Use this order:

1. First quotation mark
2. Exact quote with a starting capital and ending punctuation.
3. Last quotation marks.

The FINE Print Bring in a jar of bubbles and your children will never forget this lesson. Use pictures of famous people. Tape a famous person to the board and give him or her a quote bubble. Seeing the face with the words makes them come alive.

Activity Page – PARAGRAPH

Boo is a dog that obeys commands. This page is filled with punctuation marks for children to obey! See if your students can obey every capital, comma, quotation mark, exclamation point, and period.

PARAGRAPH

Julie trains Boo. She says, "Sit."

Boo sits. Julie says, "Stay." Boo stays.

She says, "Come!" Boo runs to her.

© 2008 Jan Z. Olsen   Handwriting Without Tears® Printing Power **55**

Tell them...
You know how to write quotations. You just did that on page 54. On this page, you are going to learn how to write quotations in a sentence. This is a paragraph that is filled with quotations and punctuation, but you're ready for it.

How do I teach this?
Review the three paragraph basics.

1. Paragraphs have topics.
Read	Paragraph aloud together.
Ask	What is the topic? (Julie training her dog Boo)

2. Paragraphs are indented.
At the board: Indent / Write **Julie trains Boo.**

3. Paragraphs have sentences.
Explain	Sentences can fit on one line or carry over onto the next line if they need more room.

— Supervise while students copy the paragraph.

Demonstrate how to write sentences with quotes.
At the board: Write   **She says, "Sit."**

Demonstrate ending punctuation inside quotes.
Write	**"Come!"**
Explain	The last line has a strong command. It uses an exclamation point. Make the **!** before the last **"** mark.

— Supervise while children to copy. (Teach every quote at board if necessary.)

Activity Page – PARAGRAPH

Have you ever thought of paintings as nouns? Nouns are names of people, places, and things. Paintings are pictures of people, places, and things. What fun! Get out the colored pencils or crayons.

REMBRANDT
by Rembrandt

YOUNG CORN
by Grant Wood

PEACHES ON A PLATE
by Renoir

Rembrandt painted self portraits.

Landscapes are pictures of land. A

painting of objects is a still life.

56 Handwriting Without Tears® *Printing Power*   © 2008 Jan Z. Olsen

Tell them...

I want to tell you about about these artists. Often artists are called by just their first or last names.
1. Rembrandt (first name) van Rijn, 1606–1669, painted many self portraits. They show him from young to old.
2. Grant Wood, 1891–1942, painted in Iowa. He is famous for *American Gothic,* a painting of a couple in front of a farm house.
3. Pierre-Auguste Renoir (last name), 1841–1919, noticed and painted how colors changed with different lighting.

How do I teach this?

Review the three paragraph basics.

1. Paragraphs have topics.

Read	Paragraph aloud together.
Ask	What is the topic? (paintings)
Say	Let's look at the pictures. What are they pictures of? People, places, and things. Have you heard of nouns? Nouns are people, places and things. People paint nouns. Ideas are nouns too. Maybe abstract painters paint ideas.

2. Paragraphs are indented.
At the board: Indent / Write **Rembrandt painted self portraits.**

3. Paragraphs have sentences.

Explain	Sentences can fit on one line or carry over onto the next line if they need more room.
Explain	The last sentence in the paragraph is written on two lines.
—	Supervise while students copy the paragraph.

The FINE Print   Use art to encourage descriptive writing. Start with portraits. Think of adjectives to describe the person's age, hair, coloring, clothing, style, expression, accessories, etc. Model the sentences for your children to copy.

Don't be surprised if this page is a hit! Compound words give children the confidence to read and write very long words.

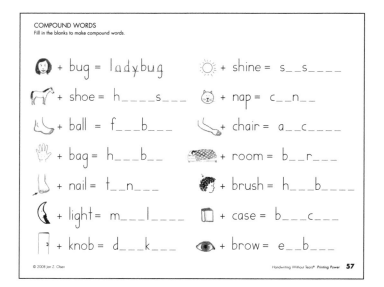

Tell them...
This is going to be fun. This page says COMPOUND WORDS. Do you know what they are? A compound word is one word made from two separate words. The pictures are taking the place of one of the two words.

How do I teach this?
Build compound words out loud with two groups.

Divide the class into two groups.

| Tell | Group 1 | You are first. Point to the picture of the lady and say **lady** |
| | Ready, go | **lady** |

| Tell | Group 2 | You are next. Point to the word bug and read **bug.** |
| | Ready, go | **bug** |

Say	Let's do it again. This time everybody say **ladybug** at the end.
	I'll point to the groups.
	Group 1	**lady**
	Group 2	**bug**
	Everybody!	**ladybug**

— Repeat with all the words.

Demonstrate how to fill in the compound words.

At the board:	Write	l _ _ _ b _ _
	Fill in	l a d y b _ _
	Fill in	l a d y b u g

— Supervise while students fill in the compound words.

The FINE Print   Think about making a class collection of compound words. Children can bring them from home or discover them in their class work. Start with **classroom.** You'll find that compound words interest children and give them confidence in spelling and reading long words.

Activity Page – WORDS

Take a vacation from school and go deep sea diving. Here are pages to enjoy and color. This page is interesting not just for the pictures, but for showing that many sea creatures have names borrowed from land animals or objects.

Tell them...

When people first named things under the sea, they often used land words. Look at the list of familiar words on the left. Now look at the sea words. See how the same words are used for things on land and in the sea.

How do I teach this?

Show how to label the pictures for words.

At the board:	Write	**c _ _**
	Fill in	**c a t**
	Say	That's how to fill in the blanks to write the words.
		If you need spelling help, there's a list at the top.

— Supervise while children fill in the labels.

Show how to label the pictures of Sea Words.

At the board	Write	**j _ _ _ _ f _ _ _**
	Ask	What should I write here? How do I spell it?
	Fill in	**j e l l y f i s h**
	Say	Finish the labels for these pictures. You can do them in any order. If you need help finding or spelling a word, use the list at the top.

— Supervise while children fill in the labels.

The FINE Print Here's some label advice: Teach children to write labels horizontally. Avoid writing on the diagonal. Directional lines may be diagonal, but not text. Text needs to be horizontal to be easy to read and write. There's another interesting label activity on workbook page 64.

Activity Page – PARAGRAPH

Here's a fun lesson about maps and geography! Political maps show state, province, and country borders—lines that are not actually on the earth. Physical maps show rivers, lakes, and mountains—things that are really there on earth. Sometimes, just looking at a political map will tell you about the physical earth. Crooked borders usually mean water.

PARAGRAPH

Look at a river on a map.

Rivers are crooked. They turn.

Lakes and coastlines are crooked.

60 Handwriting Without Tears® *Printing Power*   © 2008 Jan Z. Olsen

PARAGRAPH

COLORADO   Big Sioux River   FLORIDA   North Atlantic Ocean   North Sea

Missouri River   IOWA   Gulf of Mexico   Atlantic Ocean   UNITED KINGDOM

Mississippi River   Lake Okeechobee   Celtic Sea   English Channel

Look at borders. Rivers, lakes,

and oceans make crooked borders.

Straight lines mean dry borders.

© 2008 Jan Z. Olsen   Handwriting Without Tears® *Printing Power* 61

Tell them...
These two pages go together. They are both about land and water. Let's look at the pictures and think about where we live. Are there rivers, lakes, or oceans like that near us?

How do I teach this?
Review the three paragraph basics.
1. Paragraphs have topics.
Read	Paragraph aloud together.
Ask	What is the topic? (Page 60: rivers, lakes, and coastlines; Page 61: borders)

2. Paragraphs are indented.
At the board: Indent / Write
3. Paragraphs have sentences.
Ask	Is that the end of the sentence? No.
	Where does it end? Next line.
	Why? Sentences go to the next line if they need room.

— Supervise while students copy the paragraph.

Do a water activity on page 61.
1. Use a blue marker or crayon to outline the crooked borders.
2. Use a map, globe, or atlas.
   Find and label the crooked borders, the water names.
   Find and label the straight borders.

The FINE Print   The wonderful thing about handwriting lessons is that you can practice with so many interesting subjects. Let this two-page spread inspire you and your class. Once children know that crooked political borders are clues, they can have more fun with maps and puzzles. Pass out map pieces from a state or country puzzle. Have students trace on a piece on paper. If the piece has any crooked borders, have them find out if it means water. Have them label the borders, naming rivers, lakes, or ocean.

Activity Page – POEM

The flounder swam over from page 59! Flounders are fascinating, and this poem may be just the start of some interesting things to learn and write about.

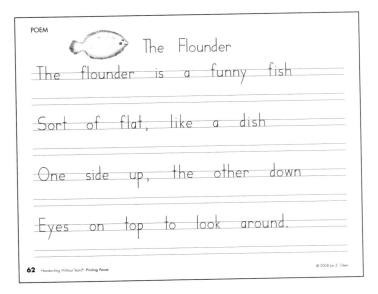

Tell them...

Flounders' eyes move, but not like our eyes. The whole eye actually moves! Flounders start out swimming like other fish with one eye on each side like other fish do. But as the flounders grow older, they live and swim as a flat fish at the bottom of the sea. An amazing thing happens. The eye on the bottom side moves to the top. That keeps the sand out of the eye and also lets the flounder look around with both eyes.

How do I teach this?

Explain the basics as they copy the poem.

1. Poems have titles.

> Read   *The Flounder* and the poem aloud together.
>
> Explain   Poems have titles. The people who write the poems write the titles.

2. Poems have lines.

> Explain   Every line starts with a capital letter.
>
> Lines are not sentences. (The first one could be, but it's not. It does not have a period.)
>
> Lines use different or no ending punctuation. (The last line often uses a period.)

3. Poems use rhyme and rhythm.

> Explain   Listen to the rhyme for lines 1 and 2: fish/dish.
>
> Listen to the rhyme for lines 3 and 4: down/around
>
> — Supervise while students copy the poem.

The FINE Print   If you have access to poetry collections and chapter story books, you can do an activity. Spread out the books and have children sort them into poetry and prose books. Then have students choose to copy a few first lines or first sentences from the books. It's also interesting for children to notice the first line index that often is found in poetry collections.

Opposites are fun and familiar. Second graders learn to call them antonyms. Experience with antonyms sharpens children's ability to observe, compare, and contrast.

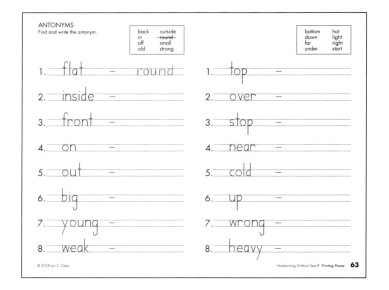

Tell them...

We are going to write antonyms—words that mean the opposite. Look at the flounder; it's not on this page. It's on the opposite page. That flounder is a flat fish. Make your hand flat on the table, like a flounder that lives on the bottom. Now lift up your hand and make it fisted like a round fish.

How do I teach this?
Demonstrate how to write opposites beside the word.

At the board: Write   **1. flat**
Ask   What word is the antonym for flat? **round**
Say   If you need help thinking of round, or spelling round, look at the word box at the top.

— Supervise while children write the antonyms.

The FINE Print   What about an independent opposite–antonym writing activity now? Or even a collaborative writing project with two students working together? Possible subjects might be: Compare a baby's room and a room for a second grader. Compare a wild animal and a family pet. Compare a farmhouse and a city apartment.

Activity Pages – LABELS AND PARAGRAPH

Your students already have written labels and paragraphs. Here's a two-page spread that does both.

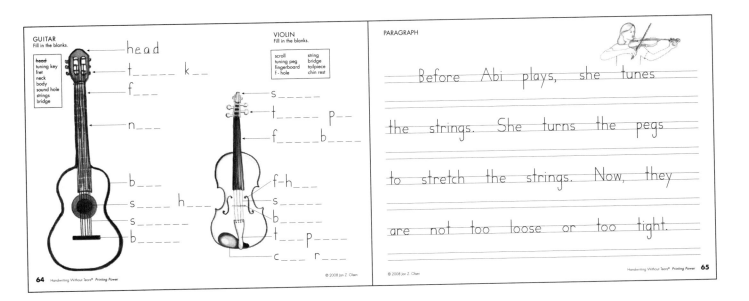

Tell them...

Guitars and violins are called string instruments. Guitars have six strings, violins have four. The instruments have different parts and different sounds. Do any of you play a guitar or violin? Do you know anyone who does?

How do I teach this?

Page 64   Explain   How to fill in the blanks using words from the list.

Remind students how to fill in the blanks using the words from the lists.

     — Supervise while children complete the labels.

Page 65

Review the three paragraph basics.

1. Paragraphs have topics.

         Read   Paragraph aloud together.

         Ask   What is the topic? (tuning strings)

         Explain   When a string is stretched just right, it is in tune. Strings have note names and are supposed to play exactly that note. Violins have different strings for these different notes: E A D G.

2. Paragraphs are indented.

      At the board: Indent / Write   **Before Abi plays, she tunes**

3. Paragraphs have sentences.

         Ask   Is that the end of the sentence? No.

                       Where does it end? Next line.

                       Why? Sentences go to the next line if they need room.

     — Supervise while students copy the paragraph.

This is a warm-up page for the next page. Do your students write name and date on papers? That is a good habit. If you're not doing that, you may want to start after this page. Show them how to write the year after the comma.

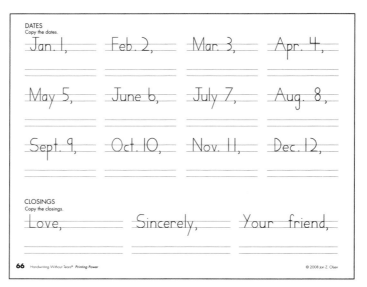

Tell them...

This is a page that will prepare you for writing a letter. It has dates, months, and days. Usually dates give the year too. At the bottom are closings. We close or end letters with a closing word or words. Then, we sign them.

How do I teach this?
Write and define abbreviation.

| At the board: | Write | **abbreviation** |
| | Explain | Abbreviation is a very long word for the short form of a word. |

Demonstrate how to read and write dates using abbreviations and commas.

At the board:	Write	**Jan. 1,**
	Explain	There are three things to notice: The capital, the period, and the comma. Capitalize months. Put a period after an abbreviation. Put a comma after the number that is the day of the date.
	Read	**Jan. 1,** out loud as **January first**.
	Explain	1. We say the long word, not the short abbreviation. 2. We read the number as first, second, third, fourth etc.

Read the months aloud as a class to notice which are abbreviated:

| | Explain | January is abbreviated, February is abbreviated, March is abbreviated, April is abbreviated, May is not, June is not, etc. |
| | — Supervise while students copy dates. | |

Show how to write   **Love,   Sincerely,   Your friend,**

| At the board: | Write | The words. Point to the capitals and commas. |
| | — Supervise while they copy the closings. | |

The FINE Print   It's fun for children to know that famous people share their birthdays. It's simple to find this on the Internet. Consider a regular writing activity to feature your birthday children. It can be as simple as, _____'s birthday is ____. It is also the birthday of _____, a famous _____.

Activity Page – THANK YOU LETTER

Writing thank you notes and letters is one of life's very important skills. Today's letter may be for a birthday gift, or a field trip tour. But in a few years, it may be after an important college or job interview. Start now.

THANK YOU LETTER
Write your own thank you letter.

Date
_____

Greeting
Dear _____

Body
Thank you _____

_____

_____

_____

Closing
Sincerely,
Signature
_____

© 2008 Jan Z. Olsen   Handwriting Without Tears® *Printing Power* **67**

Tell them...
Our bodies have parts and letters have parts. The parts of a letter have names and go in certain places.

How do I teach this?
Write and name the basic parts of a letter.

At the board: Explain   We write a letter from the top to the bottom in this order and place.
              Write   **Date**
                           Greeting,
                           Body
                           Closing,
                           Signature

Ask children to say what each part does. Write the answers.

Add   The answers that children give. Fill in what they don't know.

Date	When? The day you are writing, in month, day, and year form.
Greeting	To whom? It greets and says the person's name to whom you are writing.
Body	The message: What you want to say or tell.
Closing	Nice ending: A friendly close to the letter that suits the letter. (Love for family)
Signature	Your name: This tells who wrote the letter.

Have children write their own thank you letters.
or
Make up a thank you letter for your students to copy from the board.

At the board: Demonstrate   Each part.
              Remember   The comma in the date, after the greeting, and after the closing.

Children who see this page just want to do it. This is different and it makes children think.

LETTER - WORD FUN

Copy the letters and words. They sound the same.

B-bee,   J-jay,   I-eye,   C-sea,

Y's-wise,   U-you,   K-Kay,   P-pea,

R's-ours,   T-tea,   Y-why?   It's fun!

68 *Handwriting Without Tears® Printing Power*   © 2008 Jan Z. Olsen

Tell them...

Close your books. I just want you to listen to me read part of this page to you. (Read first line.) Now look at the page. Those letters have names that sound just like words. Capital **B** sounds like the insect bee. Capital **J** sounds like jay the bird. Capital **I** sounds like eye the body part, and capital **C** sounds like the sea that has water.

How do I teach this?

Write   **B – bee**,

Say   This is the letter capital **B**

               This is a dash

               This is the word **bee**

               This is a comma.

               Now you copy the rest of the page.

— Supervise while children copy in the workbooks.

The FINE Print   This activity is actually a sort of homonym activity, except it uses letters and words instead of just words.

Activity Page – HOMONYMS

Second grade is a big year for spelling and alphabetical order! Homonyms are perfect for sharpening those skills.

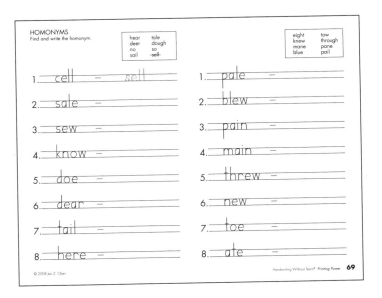

Tell them...
Homonyms are words that sound the same, but have different spellings and meanings.

How do I teach this?
Show students how to find the homonym for cell.

At the board:	Write	**cell**
	Explain	There are two meanings of cell – a prison cell, or a tiny cell in a plant or animal
	Ask	Can you think of a word that sounds like cell but has a different spelling and meaning.
		Can you find the homonym in the word bank?
	Help	Listen to this sentence. They sell popcorn at the movie.
At the board:	Write	**sell**

Give students strategies for finding homonyms.
1. Use the word bank.
2. Remember that not all homonyms start with the same letter.
3. Skip words you can't figure out.
4. Cross out word bank words as you use them. See what's left!

Activity Page – SINGLE LINE PRACTICE

Your second graders sometimes need to write on single lines. While they practice that, they can review writing items in a series. Use a colon to start a series. Use commas to separate the items. If students forget commas, you may see some emu toucans. Here's a paragraph about mammals.

SINGLE LINE PRACTICE

Copy the lists.

Birds: crow, dove, duck, emu, toucan

Fish: eel, guppy, ray, shark, tuna

Insects: ant, bee, fly, ladybug, wasp

Reptiles: alligator, lizard, snake, turtle

© 2008 Jan Z. Olsen

SINGLE LINE PRACTICE

Copy.

They swim, crawl, or fly,

but they are all mammals. Why?

Their babies drink mother's milk.

They have hair, and breathe air.

Tell them...

Page 70 is about animals, but it's a page for older students. It requires you to write on a single line and write a smaller size. You can do that. There's something else. You are going to use a colon and commas. Page 71 is about an animal group that was not on page 70. We belong to this animal group. Do you know what it is? We are mammals.

How do I teach this?

At the board: Indent / Write **Birds: crow, dove, duck, emu, toucan**

Explain   How to copy items in a series:
            1. Capitalize the title of the list
            2. Put a colon before the items in the list
            3. Put a comma and a space after each item
        — Supervise while children copy the lists.

Remind them that they will be writing on a single line and with a smaller size.
Review paragraph basics:

1. Paragraphs have topics.

Read   Paragraph aloud together.
Ask   What is the topic? (mammals)

2. Paragraphs are indented.

At the board: Indent / Write

3. Paragraphs have sentences.

Ask   Is that the end of the sentence? No.
            Where does it end? Next line.
            Why? Sentences go to the next line if they need room.
        — Supervise while students copy the paragraph.

The FINE Print   Time for science! If you really want your second graders to shine, teach them about vertebrates and invertebrates. Explain that we (mammals), birds, fish, reptiles, and amphibians have backbones or vertebrae. We can reach back and feel them. Write the words vertebrates and Invertebrates on the board. Invertebrates do not have backbones. Insects are the only animals on the page that do not have bones. They have a hard, outside covering. Second graders have strong opinions about animals. Animals are an excellent subject for informational paragraphs. Copying a paragraph like this could easily lead to writing a similar paragraph about other animal groups.

© 2008 Jan Z. Olsen

Activity Page – CAPITALS – ABOUT ME

It's easier for children to remember capitalization rules if the rules apply to them personally.

CAPITALS · ABOUT ME
Fill in the blanks about yourself.

CAPITALIZE:

My name is _____.   Names

My initials are ___. ___. ___.   Initials

Today is _____.   Days

My birthday is in _____.   Months

I speak _____.   Languages

My favorite holiday is _____.   Holidays

Days: Sunday, Monday, Tuesday, Wednesday, Thursday, Friday, Saturday
Months: January, February, March, April, May, June, July, August, September, October, November, December

72 *Handwriting Without Tears® Printing Power*   © 2008 Jan Z. Olsen

Tell them...
Each one of you is unique. There is nobody else in the world just like you. This is a personal page. You aren't going to copy. You are going to write your own information.

How do I teach this?
Go through each item, explaining how to complete the sentence and tell the capitalization rules.

My name is _____.   Write your first name here.
                                 The capital rule is: Capitalize the name of a person. Wait for children each time.

My initials are _____.   Write the capital letters that start your first, middle, and last names.
                                    The capital rule is: Capitalize a person's initials.

Today is _____.   Teachers choice:
                                 1. Write the day of the week on the board for them to copy:
                                    Monday, Tuesday, Wednesday, Thursday, Friday
                                 2. Write the abbreviation of the day of the week on the board for them to copy:
                                    Mon. Tues. Wed. Thurs. Fri.
                                 3. Write today's date for them to copy.
                                    The capital rule is: Capitalize days of the week and months of the year.

My birthday is in _____.   Write the abbreviation for the month you were born.
                                      The capital rule is: Capitalize months of the year.

I speak _____.   Write the language you speak.
                                The capital rule is: Capitalize languages.

My favorite holiday is_____.   Write the holiday.
                                        The capital rule is: Capitalize holidays.

It's easier for children to remember capitalization rules if the rules apply to them personally.

CAPITALS - ABOUT ME
Fill in the blanks about yourself.

CAPITALIZE:

My school is _____. Schools

My teacher is _____. _____. Titles, names

I read _____. Book titles

I live in _____. Cities, towns

The closest water is _____. Rivers, lakes, oceans

My friend said, "_____." First word of a quote

Titles: Mr., Miss, Ms, Mrs., Dr.
Book titles: First, last, and important words

© 2008 Jan Z. Olsen   Handwriting Without Tears® *Printing Power* **73**

Tell them...
Each one of you is unique. There is nobody else in the world just like you. This is a personal page. You aren't going to copy. You are going to write your own information.

How do I teach this?
Go through each item, explaining how to complete the sentence and tell the capitalization rules.

My school is_____.   Write the name of this school.
                            The capital rule is: Capitalize the names of schools and universities.

My teacher is _____.   Write my title and name (_____).
                            The capital rules are: Capitalize the title of a person. Capitalize the name of a person.

I read_____.   Write the title of a book you've read.
                            The capital rule is: Capitalize the first, last, and important words in a title.

I live in _____.   Write the name of our town or city.
                            The capital rule is: Capitalize the names of towns or cities.

The closest water is _____. Write _____.
                            The capital rule is: Capitalize the names of rivers, lakes, and oceans.

My friend said, "_____." Write something short that your friend said. It can be as simple as, "Hi." or "Call me." The capital rule is: Capitalize the first word of a quote.

The FINE Print   The key to these capitalization rules is that the specific name of a day, month, language, holiday, school, person, book, city, etc. is capitalized. General words like day, month, language, and holiday are not capitalized.

✓ Check Your Teaching

This unique strategy allows you to check your teaching as you go, or check your teaching at the end of it all. Because handwriting is taught through direct instruction, you can check to be sure you did a good job teaching children their letters. We divided these mini-tests by letter group. We suggest testing in very small groups or even individually. It's best when you can watch children form their letters.

Directions
1. On a blank sheet of paper, draw a single line.
2. Ask the child to print the word for the letter group you are checking (see below).
3. Spell the word(s) for the child.
4. Check their letters and spacing.
5. If there are problems, go back and review letters with the child.

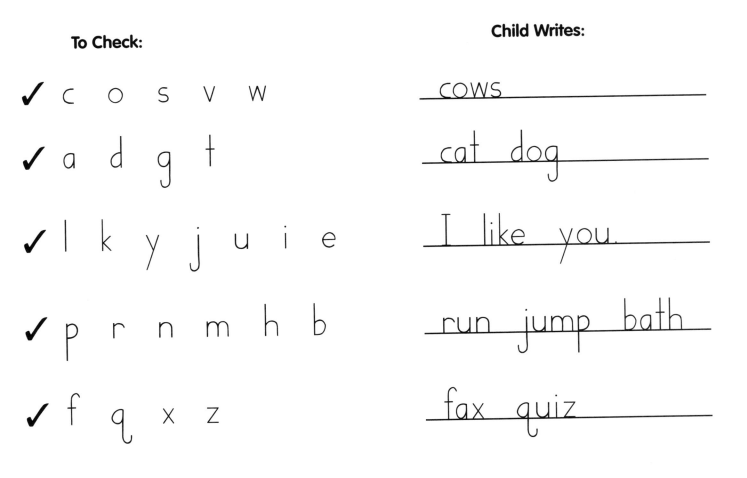

To Check:

✓ c o s v w

✓ a d g t

✓ l k y j u i e

✓ p r n m h b

✓ f q x z

Child Writes:

cows

cat dog

I like you.

run jump bath

fax quiz

To download a Check Your Teaching worksheet for giving these mini-tests by letter group or with the whole alphabet, visit **www.hwtears.com/click**.

NUMBER LESSONS

Multisensory Activities for Numbers

You will teach numbers similar to how you teach capital letters. You can use a variety of multisensory activities to support your teaching. Our three favorites are listed below. They combine to make a foolproof method of teaching numbers so children won't reverse them.

Wet–Dry–Try

Teacher's Part

Teacher demonstrates correct number formation.

Student's Part

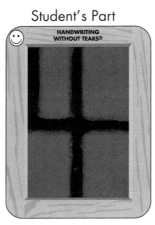

WET
- Wet a Little Sponge Cube.
- Squeeze it out.
- Trace the number with the sponge.
- Wet your finger and trace again.

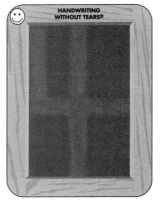

DRY
- Crumple a little paper towel.
- Dry the number a few times.
- Gently blow for final drying.

TRY
- Take a Little Chalk Bit.
- Use it to write the number

Gray Blocks

Gray Blocks are an easy transition from the Slate Chalkboard. Refer to them as "tiny pictures of the Slate," and children will transfer the Slate Chalkboard concepts beautifully. You can purchase Gray Block Paper at www.hwtears.com.

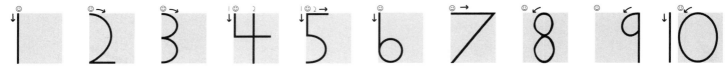

Door Tracing

The smiley face concepts are good for preventing and correcting reversals. This is a multisensory activity for large body movements. Pretend the door is a large slate or a large Gray Block and trace numbers on it. You can use a laser too. Refer to page 26 in this guide.

Try this fun game! Play the Boss of the Door. Students take turns tracing numbers in the door and guessing one another's numbers. To make math activities a little more exciting, challenge students to trace a number and have another student give a basic math question that makes that answer (e.g., the student would trace 9 and another would say "8 + 1").

Teach

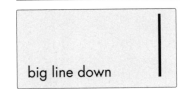

big line down

Get Started Say, "Turn to page 75. This is **I**. Watch me. I make it like this (demonstrate **I** on paper or board). Let's read these sentences, 'I can write **I**. I can count **I**.' Look, (teacher points) one football."

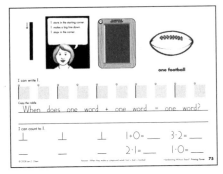

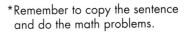

*Remember to copy the sentence and do the math problems.

Finger Trace Model Step-by-Step

Say the step-by-step directions or read the number story on the workbook page while tracing. Children watch, then trace **I**.

Copy 1

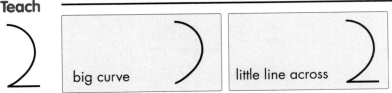

Say the step-by-step directions while demonstrating. Children watch, then copy **I**s.

Teach

2

big curve

little line across

Get Started Say, "Turn to page 76. This is **2**. Watch me. I make it like this (demonstrate **2** on paper or board). Let's read these sentences, 'I can write **2**. I can count to **2**.' Look, (teacher points) two boots."

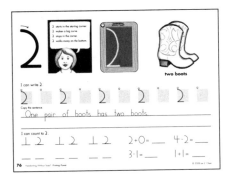

*Remember to copy the sentence and do the math problems.

Finger Trace Model Step-by-Step

2

Say the step-by-step directions or read the number story on the workbook page while tracing. Children watch, then trace **2**.

Copy 2

2 2 2 2 2

Say the step-by-step directions while demonstrating. Children watch, then copy **2**s.

Teach

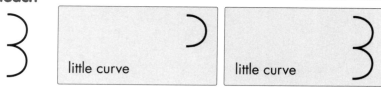

little curve	little curve

Get Started   Say, "Turn to page 77. This is **3**. Watch me. I make it like this (demonstrate **3** on paper or board). Let's read these sentences, 'I can write **3**. I can count to **3**.' Look, (teacher points) three wheels."

*Remember to copy the sentence and do the math problems.

Finger Trace Model Step-by-Step

Say the step-by-step directions or read the number story on the workbook page while tracing. Children watch, then trace **3**.

Copy 3

Say the step-by-step directions while demonstrating. Children watch, then copy **3**s.

Teach

little line down	little line across	big line down

Get Started   Say, "Turn to page 78. This is **4**. Watch me. I make it like this (demonstrate **4** on paper or board). Let's read these sentences, 'I can write **4**. I can count to **4**.' Look, (teacher points) four chairs."

*Remember to copy the sentence and do the math problems.

Finger Trace Model Step-by-Step

Say the step-by-step directions or read the number story on the workbook page while tracing. Children watch, then trace **4**.

Copy 4

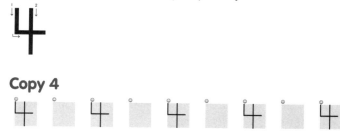

Say the step-by-step directions while demonstrating. Children watch, then copy **4**s.

Teach

5

little line down	little curve	jump little line across

Get Started Say, "Turn to page 79. This is **5**. Watch me. I make it like this (demonstrate **5** on paper or board). Let's read these sentences, 'I can write **5**. I can count to **5**.' Look, (teacher points) five fingers."

*Remember to copy the sentence and do the math problems.

Finger Trace Model Step-by-Step

5

Say the step-by-step directions or read the number story on the workbook page while tracing. Children watch, then trace **5**.

Copy 5

5 5 5 5 5

Say the step-by-step directions while demonstrating. Children watch, then copy **5**s.

Teach

6

start in corner go down	curl up in the corner

Get Started Say, "Turn to page 80. This is **6**. Watch me. I make it like this (demonstrate **6** on paper or board). Let's read these sentences, 'I can write **6**. I can count to **6**.' Look, (teacher points) six insects."

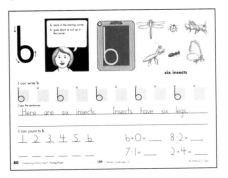

Note: We teach **6** starting in the top left corner so children do not reverse the number. It is fine for children to start in the top center once they can write **6** without reversals.

*Remember to copy the sentence and do the math problems.

Finger Trace Model Step-by-Step

6

Say the step-by-step directions or read the number story on the workbook page while tracing. Children watch, then trace **6**.

Copy 6

6 6 6 6 6

Say the step-by-step directions while demonstrating. Children watch, then copy **6**s.

Teach

7

little line across

big line
slide down

Get Started Say, "Turn to page 81. This is **7**. Watch me. I make it like this (demonstrate **7** on paper or board). Let's read these sentences, 'I can write **7**. I can count to **7**.' Look, (teacher points) seven days."

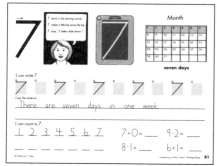

*Remember to copy the sentence and do the math problems.

Finger Trace Model Step-by-Step

Say the step-by-step directions or read the number story on the workbook page while tracing. Children watch, then trace **7**.

Copy 7

Say the step-by-step directions while demonstrating. Children watch, then copy **7**s.

Teach

8

begin with S

back up
to the top

Get Started Say, "Turn to page 82. This is **8**. Watch me. I make it like this (demonstrate **8** on paper or board). Let's read these sentences, 'I can write **8**. I can count to **8**.' Look, (teacher points) eight sides."

*Remember to copy the sentence and do the math problems.

Finger Trace Model Step-by-Step

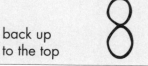

Say the step-by-step directions or read the number story on the workbook page while tracing. Children watch, then trace **8**.

Copy 8

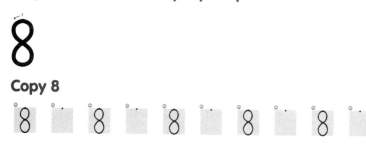

Say the step-by-step directions while demonstrating. Children watch, then copy **8**s.

 Handwriting Without Tears® 2nd Grade Printing Teacher's Guide

© 2008 Jan Z. Olsen

Teach

| little curve | up to the corner | big line down |

Get Started Say, "Turn to page 83. This is **9**. Watch me. I make it like this (demonstrate **9** on paper or board). Let's read these sentences, 'I can write **9**. I can count to **9**.' Look, (teacher points) nine gumballs."

*Remember to copy the sentence and do the math problems.

Finger Trace Model Step-by-Step

9

Say the step-by-step directions or read the number story on the workbook page while tracing. Children watch, then trace **9**.

Copy 9

9   9   9   9   9

Say the step-by-step directions while demonstrating. Children watch, then copy **9**s.

Teach

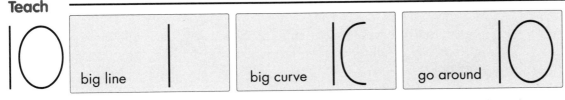

| big line | big curve | go around |

Get Started Say, "Turn to page 84. This is **10**. Watch me. I make it like this (demonstrate **10** on paper or board). Let's read these sentences, 'I can write **10**. I can count to **10**.' Look, (teacher points) ten fingers and ten toes."

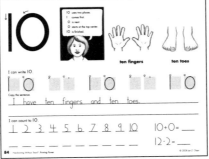

*Remember to copy the sentence and do the math problems.

Finger Trace Model Step-by-Step

10

Say the step-by-step directions or read the number story on the workbook page while tracing. Children watch, then trace **10**.

Copy 10

10   10   10   10

Say the step-by-step directions while demonstrating. Children watch, then copy **10**s.

Activity Page – NUMBER PRACTICE

Here are easy addition and subtraction problems to give simulated math practice.

NUMBER PRACTICE

Add:

0 + 1 = ___   1 + 1 = ___   2 + 1 = ___   3 + 1 = ___   4 + 1 = ___

Subtract:

7 - 1 = ___   8 - 1 = ___   9 - 1 = ___   10 - 1 = ___   11 - 1 = ___

Add:

0	1	2	3	4	5	6	7	8	9
+1	+1	+1	+1	+1	+1	+1	+1	+1	+1

Subtract:

2	3	4	5	6	7	8	9	10	11
-1	-1	-1	-1	-1	-1	-1	-1	-1	-1

© 2008 Jan Z. Olsen   Handwriting Without Tears® *Printing Power* **85**

Tell them...
You have finished all the numbers up to 10. Let's try these easy math questions for some more number practice.

How do I teach this?

Explain There are two ways to write math problems. We can write them horizontally like this → or vertically like this ↓. This page uses both.

At the board: **Write**   **0 + 1 = 1**

Say   This math problem has a line for the answer. Be sure that the numbers you write bump the lines.

Write

$$0$$
$$\underline{+\ 1}$$
$$1$$

Say   This problem does not give a line for the answer. I just write the answer under the problem. I make my answer the same size as the numbers in the problem. When you use math papers, try to make your numbers the same size as the problem uses.

— Supervise as students complete the problems.

How do I help children with number reversals?
Despite your good teaching and these workbook pages, some children forget what they've learned when they are using worksheets or writing numbers on other papers. Use this friendly strategy:
1. Check arithmetic or "counting" papers.
2. Mark only one reversal per paper. Mark the lowest number. Ignore all other reversals.
3. Show the child how to make the one reversed number correctly with the slate or Gray Block.

Gradually all reversals will be eliminated. You will always teach the lowest number and it will get all the help it needs. With this technique, you can easily and happily eliminate all reversals.

Activity Page – FINAL CHECK

You're busy and it's tricky to track 26 lowercase letters when you have 20 to 26 children! This page will help you.

FINAL CHECK

Name_____ Date_____

☐ Write and check the capital alphabet.

A _ _ _ _ _ _ _ _ _ _ _ _ _

_ _ _ _ _ _ _ _ _ _ _ _ _

☐ Write and check the lowercase alphabet.

a _ _ _ _ _ _ _ _ _ _ _ _ _

_ _ _ _ _ _ _ _ _ _ _ _ _

☐ Write and check the numbers.

1 _ _ _ _ _ _ _ _ _

86   Handwriting Without Tears® *Printing Power*   © 2008 Jan Z. Olsen

---

Tell them...

Look at this! It's the last page in the book. It's your job to print the 26 capital and 26 lowercase letters. See the capital **A** and the lowercase **a**. The capital is tall. All capitals are tall. Lowercase **a** is small. But not all lowercase letters are small. Some are tall and some are descending; they go below the line.

How do I teach this?

Say   Write the capitals, the lowercase letters, and the numbers.
         Use the size of the model to help you decide what size to make the letters and numbers.
         Do your best printing.

To use this page for formal assessment:

You may choose to give this page to children as a small assessment of their skills. You will give it to them individually and observe their letter/number start and formations. Watch students write every letter/number. You may verbally dictate the letters for them so you have time to observe and mark their symbols.

Place a small **1** at the start and then tiny arrows with additional numbers to indicate the direction of their strokes. You only need to mark letters that are started or formed incorrectly.

When you finish, you can observe students' work and determine who needs a review of certain letters, numbers, or letter groups.

The FINE Print   Take a bow! This page will help you see how well your children are writing. This page can also help you put a final polish on their printing skills. As you review this page, you'll spot individual children or individual letters calling out for some extra attention.

HANDWRITING ADVICE
Identifying Handwriting Difficulties

As discussed in the beginning of this guide, your students may come with very different levels of writing proficiency. This section is especially important for those who enter your room less prepared. Think in terms of the eight skills required for speed and legibility (page 7). If you break the handwriting processes into these skills, it is easier to identify and correct difficulties. Use the tips below to guide your approach when helping a child who is behind in handwriting. Often the printing skills are fine, but the physical approach to handwriting or the child's interest in self-correction may need some adjustments. If you believe that the difficulty stems from something other than just a lack of instruction, consult an occupational therapist.

Below are some of the things to look for to identify where a child needs help. On the pages that follow, we include strategies for addressing specific difficulties.

PHYSICAL APPROACH

Handedness
- Switches hands while writing
- Switches hands between activities

Pencil Grip
- Holds pencil vertically
- Wraps thumb around fingers
- Uses an awkward grip
- Holds pencil with an open hand

Pencil Pressure
- Presses too hard
- Presses too lightly

Paper Placement
- Positions paper incorrectly for handedness

Posture
- Slouches in chair
- Has head on table
- Slumps

Helper Hand
- Moves paper when writing
- Places helping hand incorrectly

SELF CORRECTION
Erasing/Editing
- Erases too much
- Works carelessly

PRINTING SKILLS

Memory
- Misses letters or numbers in assignments
- Confuses capital and lowercase letters
- Writes unidentifiable letters/numbers

Orientation
- Reverses letters or numbers

Placement
- Misplaces certain letters or numbers
- Uses wrong lines

Size
- Makes letter size too big for grade level papers

Start
- Writes letters/numbers from the bottom
- Starts with the wrong part or on the wrong side

Sequence
- Forms letters that are not standard
- Makes letter strokes out of order

Spacing
- Puts too much space between letters in words
- Runswordstogether

Control
- Makes misshapen letters/numbers

Remediating Handwriting Difficulties

The remediation strategies here can help you correct handwriting difficulties. Additionally, parents often ask about ways they too can assist their child. This section gives you remediation tips and information for parents.

When facilitating handwriting remediation, remember the following:

Notice what's right: Recognition of what's right is encouraging and should come before any suggestions or corrections. You can give this easy handwriting check to your students to see if they learned what you taught them. Use it after teaching each letter group, or give it to students all at once to see what they already know and what they need.

On a blank sheet of paper, draw a single line and have the child write:

cows
cat   dog
I like you.
run   jump   bath
fax   quiz

A Click Away
hwtears.com/click

Make sure you mark each letter with numbers and arrows to show how it was made. You may spell the words for children.

Keep practice short: Ten or fifteen minutes is long enough. You want the child's full attention and optimum effort during the lesson. Then end the lesson while it's still going well or the minute you've lost the child's interest.

Use imitation: What is imitation? It is watching someone do something first, then doing it yourself. With imitation, the child has the opportunity to see how a letter is written; to see the actual movements which were responsible for making the mark. Then the child can associate the mark with the movement that produced it. This is crucial because we are as concerned with how a letter is formed as we are with how the end product looks. Imitation has two advantages:
1. It gives the child the best chance to write the letter.
2. It teaches the child the correct motor habits.

We are convinced that imitation has been neglected and should be rediscovered with appreciation.

Communicate: Share helpful secrets with others. If you want to help a child with handwriting, the best thing you can do is to get everyone on the same page. As long as everyone knows what is needed, you can move the remediation along. Use the Handwriting All Year ideas on page 132 to send mini homework assignments home.

Consistency and Follow-Through: Identify the problems, set-up the team, and let the progress begin. If you are consistent, you will see progress in the child's handwriting.

Help Others: You may develop a love for helping children with handwriting. With HWT workshop training and the HWT program, you can become HWT Level I Certified. Visit www.hwtcertification.com.

STRATEGIES FOR A PHYSICAL APPROACH
Handedness
By the time formal handwriting training begins, it's important for a child to have developed hand dominance. Sometimes you have to help the child choose the more skilled hand and then facilitate use of that hand. Collaborate with parents, teachers, therapists, and other significant individuals in the child's life to determine the more skilled hand. Create a checklist of activities for everyone to observe (brushing teeth, eating, dressing, cutting, etc.). Together, you can position materials on the preferred side, and encourage use of the most skilled hand for handwriting.

Pencil Grip

Demonstration
Always demonstrate the correct hold and finger positions. Use the Pencil Pick-Up activity on page 54 in this guide and sing the *Picking Up My Pencil* song, Track 9 on the *Rock, Rap, Tap & Learn* CD.

Correct pencil grip in three easy steps
You can help a child develop a correct pencil grip or fix one that is awkward. The trick is that you don't teach grip by itself. Teach grip in three stages, and you will be impressed with how easy it becomes. The technique takes consistency and a little time. (See page 40 for an illustration of correct grips.) Tell children that you are going to show them a new way to hold their pencil, but that they are not allowed to use the new grip for their writing (yet).

1. Pick-Up—Have students pick up their pencils and hold them in the air with the fingers and thumbs correctly placed. Help position their fingers if necessary. Tell your students, "Wow, that is a perfect pencil grip. Now make a few circles in the air with the perfect pencil grip. Drop it and do it again." Repeat this 5 times a day for a couple of weeks.

2. Scribble-wiggle—Give students a piece of paper with five randomly placed dots. Have them pick up their pencils, hold them correctly, and put their pencil point on the dot. The little finger side of the pencil hand rests on the paper. Students make wiggly marks through and around the dot without lifting their pencils or hands. (The helping hand is flat and holds the paper.) The advantage of this step is that children develop their pencil grip and finger control without being critical of how the writing looks. Do this daily for a couple weeks.

3. Write—Have students pick up the pencil, hold it correctly, and write the first letter of their names. Add letters until the children can write their names easily with the correct grip. Once they are writing letters with their new grip, grant them permission to use it for all their writing.

Drive the Pencil Trick

(This is a summary of a tip from Betsy Daniel, COTA/L and Christine Bradshaw, OTR/L.) Name the fingers: The thumb is the dad, and the index finger is the mom. The remaining fingers are the child and any brothers, sisters, friends, or pets. Say the pencil is the car. Just as in a real car, dad and mom sit in front and the kids, friends, or pets sit in back. For safe driving, dad shouldn't sit on mom's lap (thumb on top of index finger), and mom never sits on dad's lap (index finger on top of thumb)! If children use an overlapping or tucked-in thumb, remind them that no one can sit on anyone's lap while driving!

Adaptive Devices
If a child continues to have difficulty holding the pencil, there are a variety of grips available at school supply stores, art/stationary stores, and catalogs. Their usefulness varies from grip-to-grip and child-to-child. Experiment with them, and use them only if they make it easier for the child to hold the pencil correctly. With young children, physical devices should not be used as substitutes for physical demonstration.

Rubber Band Trick: Check the angle of the pencil. If it's standing straight up, the pencil will be hard to hold and will cause tension in the fingertips. Put a rubber band around the child's wrist. Loop another rubber band to the first one. Pull the loop over the pencil eraser. This may keep the pencil pulled back at the correct angle. You may make or buy a more comfortable version that uses ponytail holders.

Reward a Grip

Sometimes young children need motivation to use their new grip. You can offer them a small reward for remembering how to hold their pencils correctly. Track their progress so they can see how close they are to reaching their reward. Attach a photo of their correct pencil grip with a small strip of paper to their desks and stamp them every time you catch them holding their pencil correctly. Thus you help them build a good motor pattern.

Check My Grip	Look at me, I'm holding my pencil correctly.

My reward is:

① ② ③ ④ ⑤
⑥ ⑦ ⑧ ⑨ ⑩

Pencil Pressure

Sometimes children have to learn to judge and moderate their pencil pressure. It's more common for a child to push too hard than not hard enough. Regardless, both can cause problems.

Too hard: Try a mechanical pencil so the child has to control the amount of pressure. You can also have children place the paper on a mouse pad (if they press too hard they will poke holes in their paper).*

Too soft: Have the child pencil in small shapes until they are black. Use pencils with softer lead.

*Suggestions should be tried at home before they're used at school, because remedies for pencil pressure problems can be frustrating to the child.

Posture

Children will sacrifice all stability for mobility. They love to move! Children need to sit in their chairs with their hips, knees, and feet at a 90-degree angle. Check the furniture size. The chair and desk should fit the child. If you can't find a smaller chair, place something (a phone book, box, etc.) under the child's feet for stability. This will help them to sit up when it's time to write.

Helper Hand

Where is the helping hand; the hand that isn't holding the pencil? We've all seen helping hands in laps, twirling hair, or propping up foreheads. You can nag the child, but you'll get better results if you talk directly to the hand! Try it! Take the child's helping hand in yours and pretend to talk to that hand.

Name the helping hand. For example: Ask John what other name he likes that starts with **J**. If John says "Jeremy," tell him that you are going to name his helping hand "Jeremy." Have a little talk with Jeremy, the helping hand. Tell Jeremy that he's supposed to help by holding the paper. Say that John is working really hard on his handwriting, but he needs Jeremy's help. Show Jeremy where he's supposed to be. Tell John that he might have to remind Jeremy about his job.

Kids think this is a hoot. They don't get embarrassed because it's the helping hand, not them, that is being corrected. It's not John who needs to improve, it's Jeremy. This is a face-saving, but effective, reminder. Flat fingers please! A flat (but not stiff) helping hand promotes relaxed writing. Put your hand flat on the table and try to feel tension—there isn't any! Make a fist and feel the tension! Children can get uptight while writing, but a flat helping hand decreases tension.

STRATEGIES FOR SELF-CORRECTION

Sometimes children are fine with handwriting but they over- or under-correct their work. You can download The Eraser Challenge and Spot Good Writing at **www.hwtears.com/click**.

www.hwtears.com/click

The Eraser Challenge

Some children spend a lot of time erasing. Those who erase often tend to be slow and lag behind in their work. If you want to control the amount of erasing without taking away erasers, strike a deal using the following strategy:

1. Download the Eraser Flags.
2. Tape them to your students' desks or send them home for parents to use when helping with homework.
3. Every time children erase, they pull a flag.
4. Play a game by challenging children to have a certain amount of flags left at the end of the day.

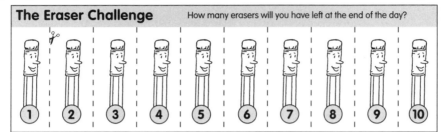

The Eraser Challenge — How many erasers will you have left at the end of the day?

Spot Good Writing

Some children have good handwriting skills but don't carry them over into general school work. Make your expectations clear and make children accountable. Download and print these notes to help children improve what's good and what's not.

SPOT GOOD WRITING

Can you check all of these?
- Strokes - start, sequence of letters good
- Sit letters on line
- Size of letters seems suitable
- Spaces in sentences
- Start with a CAPITAL
- Stop with a ? !
- See if others can read

Handwriting Without Tears®   © 2008 Jan Z. Olsen

Spacing

Teach your students to put letters in a word close to each other. Have them put their index fingers up and bring them close together, without touching. Tell them, "In a word, the letters are close, but don't touch." Draw fingers for them.

Sentence Spacing with Pennies

Give your children pennies or chips to use. Teach them how to look at a short simple sentence and fix the pennies to match as in this example.

I   SEE   A   DOG.

Sick Sentence Clinic

The teacher writes a sentence with the letters too far apart. Circle each word in the sentence. Now copy the sentence over, putting the letters closer. For example:

   I a m b i g.   I am big.

Now, write a sentence with the letters too close. Children underline each word in the sentence. Leave space between words. Now copy the sentence over with spaces between the words.

   Icanrun.   I can run.

The Nothing Bottle

If students run their words together:

Say that you will give them what they need for spaces. Have them hold out their hands to catch it. Take a huge empty bottle (or any container) and make a big show of pouring into their hands. Ask, "What did you get?" Nothing! Tell them to put nothing after every word they write.

Nothing Bottle

STRATEGIES FOR PRINTING SKILLS

Memory
- Play visual memory games with capital and lowercase flashcards.
- Use HWT readiness materials (Wood Pieces Set, Capital Letter Cards, Stamp and See Screen™) with the *Pre-K Teacher's Guide* and *Kindergarten Teacher's Guide*.
- Go on letter scavenger hunts. Look for things around the school or house that begin with letters that need to be practiced.
- Build a letter card repertoire. Start with just the letters that the child can name instantly. Add one new letter at a time.

Orientation
- Correct number reversals by choosing one reversal per assignment. If children reverse many of their numbers, work on them one at a time beginning with the lowest number. Master that formation before moving on to another number.
- Use Wet–Dry–Try. The Slate Chalkboard works for capitals and number reversals; the Blackboard with Double Lines is for lowercase. See page 24 of this guide.
- Play the Mystery Letter game using Gray Blocks or Slate.

Placement
- Teach bumping the lines using the Blackboard with Double Lines and Wet–Dry–Try. See page 25 of this guide.
- Mark scores on a baseline.
- Do demonstration/imitation of small, tall, descending letter placement.
- Do letter size, page 30 of this guide, followed by writing letters or words on double lines.
- Model how different paper is used and how letters sit on the lines.

Size
- Use paper that promotes an age–appropriate letter size.
- Avoid poorly designed worksheets: overly busy, confusing lines, inadequate room for writing.
- Use landscape rather than portrait worksheets.

Start/Sequence
- Demonstrate/imitate to build correct habits for letters.
- Teach the TOP! See page 16 of this guide.
- Use ☺ cue to help children notice the top left corner.
- Use Slate Chalkboard with Wet–Dry–Try, page 24 of this guide.
- Use Gray Block Paper.

Spacing
- Teach spacing actively.
- Use worksheets that model generous spacing: horizontal, landscape format if possible.
- Use the *Sentence Song* on the *Rock, Rap, Tap & Learn* CD, Track 7.
- Use Sentence Spacing with Pennies, page 130 of this guide.
- Teach children about spacing using their fingers, page 130 of this guide.
- Teach the Sick Sentence Clinic, page 130 of this guide.
- Use the Nothing Bottle activity, page 130 of this guide.

Control
- Correct children's other printing skills to help improve their control.
- Turn to the next page for tips if you suspect the teaching method has caused problems with control.
- Consult an occupational therapist if you suspect that control is affected by a fine motor problem (clue: all other skills are okay, but control is poor).

STRATEGIES FOR OTHER METHODS AND HOME PRACTICE

Other Methods

Children in your classroom may have learned other styles of handwriting. Support and accept other styles, but only if they work. If a particular style is giving a child problems with speed or neatness, you will have to decide whether to modify or reteach it.

Typically, scripted print is something that can be modified. For example, you can teach children to eliminate unnecessary tails on letters that may be causing problems. You can even take away the slant.

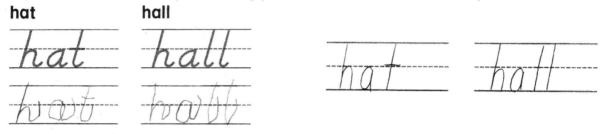

If the style is delaying the child's academics, then it might be in the child's best interest to re-teach. For example, children often will make capitals with a continuous stroke. If they can't retrace well or stay on the line, you may need to re-teach the letter using a more developmentally appropriate approach.

Continuous Stroke Capitals

Re-taught using HWT Frog Jump Strategies

Handwriting All Year

What do you do when the workbook is complete? You continue with short lessons to maintain and improve printing skills. You might like to follow a weekly routine. We have ideas for every day of the week. Here are just a few:

Monday: Capital Letters Try a Capital – Country activity.
Have children write the name of a country that begins with the first letter of their names.

Tuesday: Lowercase Letters
Sing *Descending Letters*, track 19, on the *Rock, Rap, Tap & Learn* CD. Write words with **g j y p** or **q**.

Wednesday: Words
Learn some Greek and Latin words. Write the word, the English meaning, and an English word that uses the Latin/Greek word. For example: port = carry → portable

Thursday: Sentences
Write Subject – Verb sentences. Display a group of subject words and a group of verb words from your word wall. Let children make up their own sentences. Remind them about capitals, spacing, and ending punctuation.

Friday: Fun and Numbers
Use silly fill-in-the-blanks stories. Read each other's or do them together.

EXTRAS
Here we include a few final things to facilitate good handwriting instruction.

Report Card Insert
Some report cards don't have a place to grade or mark handwriting success. This is particularly important in the lower grades because handwriting performance can affect other academic subjects. If your report card doesn't allow space for handwriting, use this downloadable form and include it with your students' report cards. It will demonstrate that you value handwriting and are monitoring progress.

Handwriting Report	Name				
Printing Skill	**Q1**	**Q2**	**Q3**	**Q4**	**Comments**
Forms capitals correctly					
Forms lowercase correctly					
Forms numbers correctly					
Writes on lines					
Writes appropriate size					
Applies skills					

Educating Others
Because handwriting often takes a back seat in today's elementary schools, it's wonderful for someone knowledgeable in handwriting, specifically the Handwriting Without Tears® method, to step forward and share that knowledge with others. Whether you are educating parents at a back-to-school night or presenting in front of a language arts committee, the information you share will improve the likelihood that others will recognize the importance of teaching handwriting.

Parents
Educate parents about HWT, pencil grip, and printing skills. Giving parents letter/number charts at the start of school helps them understand how to form letters and help their child at home. You can find parent articles to print and distribute on the website.

Colleagues
Share your HWT knowledge with your friends and co-workers. If you have attended or plan to attend our workshops, tell friends about it, or—better yet—invite them to come along. Often, all it takes is one teacher from a school getting excited about handwriting to inspire an entire school to learn more.

Administrators and Committees
Principals can be your biggest advocates. Share the information you have learned with principals and other administrators. Discuss the benefits of handwriting consistency and how HWT can help. Many HWT advocates have successfully written proposals, initiated handwriting pilot studies, presented to language arts committees, and seen large districts adopt HWT district wide. Email or call us for help - janolsen@hwtears.com or 301-263-2700. We will send you a CD loaded with everything you need to help others understand that handwriting should be an easy victory for children and how using Handwriting Without Tears® enables that success.

A Taste of Cursive!

We can't end this guide without a mention of cursive.

Second graders have a unique interest in cursive that can be to our advantage. Children who are motivated to learn new skills will pay attention. It's a grand opportunity for us to instill some habits that students will remember later. Cursive at the second grade level is tricky. Typically, students aren't ready for it until later in the school year. But, we don't want to teach something that may be forgotten over the summer. Below are some things you can do to offset the cursive curiosity and instill a few good habits without teaching the full curriculum.

First, it's important to understand a few things about our unique cursive style.

HWT CURSIVE STYLE

HWT uses a simple, continuous, vertical stroke that is easy for children to learn. The HWT letter style is also familiar because it looks like the letters and words children see and read every day. The continuous stroke style prevents reversals and prepares children for a smooth transition to cursive.

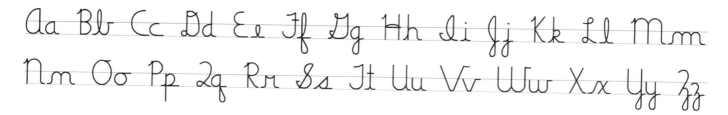

Advantages of the HWT Style

Less is more

Teaching letters with flamboyant start-up and ending strokes complicates the letter and makes letter connections more difficult. Twenty-two letters in cursive end on the bottom line and four (**o w b v**) end on the top line. Teaching children an exaggerated bottom line start-up stroke makes it difficult for them to be able to form connections with the four letters that do not end on the bottom line. Take a look at this style comparison and you will see why children like learning HWT cursive so much—it is easier to read and write.

Old-Fashioned Cursive   **Handwriting Without Tears®**

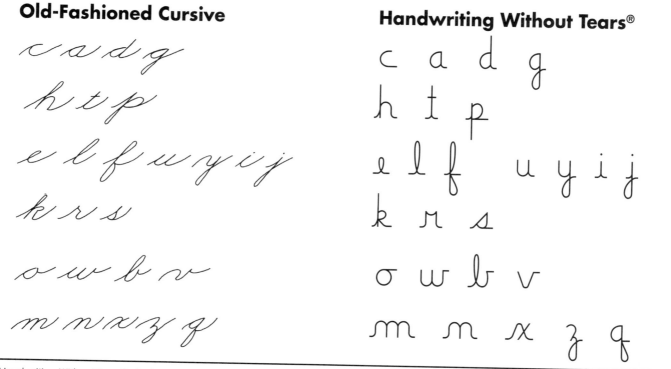

Only loopty loo when it helps you

The exaggerated beginnings and endings of difficult letters have been removed. The curlicues, fancy loops and humps, and difficult strokes are gone. This style is easy for the children to learn. For example: If you put a loop on an **h** or **k**, the law of motion takes over. As the pencil curves down, it wants to keep going away.

Cursive **h** and **k** tend to look like a letter **l** with a hump. The HWT **h** and **k** have no loops. They are neat and easy to write.

The HWT ℓ **l** and ℓ have loops it's desirable to have motion away from the letter

Our Slant on Slant

Removing the slant from cursive:

1. Easier to learn
2. Easier to write
3. Easier to read
4. Easier to develop fluency and a personal style

Are we breaking a rule?

Slanting to the right is standard practice that probably developed because of old fashioned pens. Have you ever used an old fashioned pen, a dip or quill pen? If you have, you know that when you try to make an upstroke (from bottom to top) the pen catches and splatters ink. Those pens are fine for vertical downstrokes, but upstrokes have to be slanted. Because upstrokes are an integral part of cursive (in going from the ending place of one letter to the starting place of the next), they affected the way cursive was written. Cursive and slanting went together. But today, in the era of pencils and ball point pens, slant is unnecessary. A vertical style is an easier option for teaching cursive. We aren't breaking a rule; we're making something easier for children.

Learn cursive with ease and without the slant

It makes sense that vertical cursive is easier for children.

- The vertical line is developmentally easier than the slanted line, both to perceive and to copy. Check the seminal work of Dr. Arnold Gessell on design copying.*

| — ○ + □ △

- Vertical letters in cursive are easier for children to recognize.
- It is one less thing to do. When learning cursive, children must learn new letter formations and connections. There is no reason to complicate the learning process with a superfluous slant.
- It doesn't look so scary. Vertical cursive has a manageable appearance.

*Gesell, Arnold, and others. *The First Five Years of Life.* New York: Harper and Row. 1940.

Four Simple Connections

This is all you need to connect one letter to the next. Children grasp our concepts easily.

Baseline Connections

- Occur after 22 letters
- Baseline to baseline connection – easy

- Baseline to high connection – tricky

High Connections

- Occur after 4 letters – σ w b v
- High to high connection – easy

- High to low connection – tricky (low has to be cranked up)

INTRODUCTORY CURSIVE
Teaching Baseline Letters & Connections

You can give children a taste of cursive by teaching them letters that are similar to print. The only connection you will teach is the baseline to baseline. See above. We have prepared some introductory cursive instruction for you available online. Please read the information thoroughly before giving your students a "Taste of Cursive"!

Preparation
Download and read introductory cursive information. Download and print student activities.

Directions
1. Choose one day a week to give your students a Taste of Cursive.
2. Say, "Next year you will formally learn cursive, but I can introduce some to you now."
3. Teach students one or two letters a week until the end of the school year.
4. Download activities from **www.hwtears.com/click** so your students can participate.

Skills Developed
- Translating print to cursive using letters that are similar
- Good understanding of baseline to baseline connections
- Cursive language

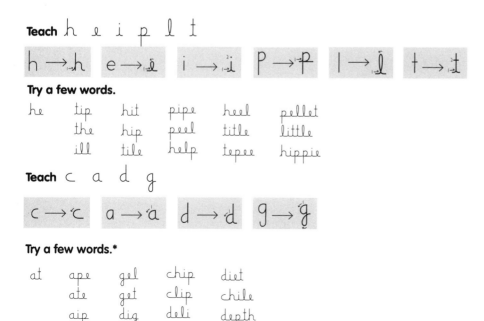

*Children will write only words that start with these letters. Using these letters in words requires a more challenging connection.

Teach ᴍ ᴍ

m → ᴍ   n → ᴺ

Try a few words.

me   him   ant   time   them
am   hen   aim   lime
an   gem   aid   then

Teach u y

u → ᵁu   y → ᵞy

Teach them these words.

my   timely
yummy

Don't teach these letters Ꮟ f j k σ q ᴙ ᴧ v ᴡ x ᴣ

Teaching Name

Teaching children their name in cursive is a nice way to present cursive and show them what they can anticipate. You will need to model connections for your students based on their name.

Preparation

Download the Name Worksheet from **www.hwtears.com/click**. Read the detailed instructions included with the download.

Directions

1. Discuss writing names in cursive.
2. Tell children to circle letters in their name.
3. Walk around the room and model the formation for each student.
4. Children practice their name.

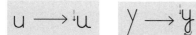

My Cursive Name
Circle the letters in your last name.

a B C D E F H I J K L M

N O P Q R S J U V W X Y Z

a b c d e f g h i j k l m

n o p q r s t u v w x y z

Teacher models last name:

Student imitates last name:

Teaching Guidelines

The HWT curriculum is highly adaptable and can be used in a number of ways. If you are looking for a completely structured approach, we created these guidelines to help you along. For faster-paced instruction, skip review lessons.*

Week	Monday	Tuesday	Wednesday	Thursday	Friday	Friday Numbers (during Math)
1 Pre-writing	Where Do You Start Your Letters? & Sign In Activity TG2nd pg.16-17	Posture & Paper TG2nd pg. 36-38 Grip TG2nd pg. 40-41	Where Do You Start Your Letters? & Sign In Activity TG2nd pg. 16-17	Posture & Paper TG2nd pg. 36-38 Grip TG2nd pg. 40-41	Where Do You Start Your Letters? & Sign In Activity TG2nd pg.16-17	*Number Review PP pg. 13 TG2nd pg. 59
2 Capitals	Frog Jump Capitals with Grey Blocks TG2nd pg. 55 PP pg. 9	Frog Jump Capitals with Double Lines TG2nd pg. 55 PP pg. 9	Frog Jump Capitals Mystery Letter Game TG2nd pg. 55 PP pg. 9	Starting Corner Capitals with Grey Blocks TG2nd pg. 56 PP pg. 10	Starting Corner Capitals with Double Lines TG2nd pg. 56 PP pg. 10	Number 1 TG2nd pg. 119 PP pg. 75
3	Center Starting Capitals with Grey Blocks TG2nd pg. 57 PP pg. 11	Center Starting Capitals with Double Lines TG2nd pg. 57 PP pg. 11	Capital Review TG2nd pg. 58 PP pg. 12	Posture & Paper TG2nd pg. 36-38 Grip TG2nd pg. 40-41	Capital Review TG2nd pg. 58 PP pg. 12	Number 2 TG2nd pg. 119 PP pg. 76
4 Lowercase	Capital Partners: Cc Oo Ss Vv Ww TG2nd pg. 60 PP pg. 14	Lowercase: t TG2nd pg. 61 PP pg. 15	Word Practice: t TG2nd pg. 61 PP pg. 15	Lowercase: a, d, g TG2nd pg. 63-65 PP pg. 16-18	*Review Letters c, o, s, v, w, t, a, d, g	Number 3 TG2nd pg. 120 PP pg. 77
5	Activity Page: Silly Spelling TG2nd pg. 66 PP pg. 19	Activity Page: Punctuation TG2nd pg. 67 PP pg. 20	Lowercase: u, i, e TG2nd pg. 68-70 PP pg. 21-23	Word Pages: u, i, e TG2nd pg. 68-70 PP pg. 21-23	Activity Page: Letter Size & Place TG2nd pg. 71 PP pg. 24	Number 4 TG2nd pg. 120 PP pg. 78
6	Activity Page: Rhyming Words TG2nd pg. 72 PP pg. 25	Lowercase: l, k TG2nd pg. 73-74 PP pg. 26-27	Word Pages: l, k TG2nd pg. 73-74 PP pg. 26-27	Activity Page: Capitals, Commas TG2nd pg. 75 PP pg. 28	Activity Page: Paragraph TG2nd pg. 76 PP pg. 29	Number 5 TG2nd pg. 121 PP pg. 79
7	Lowercase: y, j TG2nd pg. 77-78 PP pg. 30-31	Word Pages: y, j TG2nd pg. 77-78 PP pg. 30-31	*Review Letters u, i, e, l, k, y, j	Activity Page: Singular/Plural TG2nd pg. 79 PP pg. 32	Activity Page: Paragraph TG2nd pg. 80 PP pg. 33	Number 6 TG2nd pg. 121 PP pg. 80
8	Lowercase: p, r TG2nd pg. 82-83 PP pg. 34-35	Word Pages: p, r TG2nd pg. 82-83 PP pg. 34-35	Lowercase: n, m TG2nd pg. 84-85 PP pg. 36-37	Word Pages: n, m TG2nd pg. 84-85 PP pg. 36-37		Number 7 TG2nd pg. 122 PP pg. 81
9	Lowercase: h, b TG2nd pg. 86-87 PP pg. 38-39	Word Page: h, b TG2nd pg. 86-87 PP pg. 38-39	*Review Letters p, r, n, m, h, b	Activity Page: Turn h Into b TG2nd pg. 88 PP pg. 40	Activity Page: Word Search TG2nd pg. 89 PP pg. 41	Number 8 TG2nd pg. 122 PP pg. 82

Week	Monday	Tuesday	Wednesday	Thursday	Friday	Friday Numbers (during Math)
10	**Lowercase: f, q** TG2nd pg. 90-91 PP pg. 42-43	**Word Pages: f, q** TG2nd pg. 90-91 PP pg. 42-43	**Activity Page: Paragraph** TG2nd pg. 92 PP pg. 44	**Activity Page: Latin Greek** TG2nd pg. 93 PP pg. 45		**Number 9** TG2nd pg. 123 PP pg. 83
11	**Lowercase: x, z** TG2nd pg. 94-95 PP pg. 46-47	**Word Pages: x, z** TG2nd pg. 94-95 PP pg. 46-47	***Review Letters f, q, x, z**	**Activity Page: Lowercase Review** TG2nd pg. 96 PP pg. 48		**Number 10** TG2nd pg. 123 PP pg. 84
12 Review Week	***Review Frog Jump Capitals F, E, D, P, B, R, N, M**	***Review Starting Corner Capitals H, K, L, U, V, W, X, Y, Z**	***Review Center Starting Capitals C, O, Q, S, A, I, T, J**	***Review Capital Partners c, o, s, v, w, t**	***Review High Frequency Letters a, d, g**	**Activity Page: Number Practice** TG2nd pg. 124 PP pg. 85
13 Review & Activity Pages	***Review Lowercase: u, i, e, l, k, y, j**	***Review Diver Letters: p, r, n, m, h, b**	***Review Lowercase f, q, x, z**	***Review Numbers**	**Sentence Page** TG2nd pg. 97 PP pg. 49	
14 Activity Pages	**Sentence Page** TG2nd pg. 98 PP pg. 50	**Sentence Page** TG2nd pg. 98 PP pg. 51	**Paragraph** TG2nd pg. 99 PP pg. 52	**Poem** TG2nd pg. 100 PP pg. 53	**Quotations** TG2nd pg. 101 PP pg. 54	
15 Activity Pages	**Paragraph** TG2nd pg. 102 PP pg. 55	**Paragraph** TG2nd pg. 103 PP pg. 56	**Compound Words** TG2nd pg. 104 PP pg. 57	**Words** TG2nd pg. 105 PP pg. 58-59	**Paragraph** TG2nd pg. 106 PP pg. 60	
16 Activity Pages & Review	**Paragraph** TG2nd pg. 106 PP pg. 61	**Poem** TG2nd pg. 107 PP pg. 62	***Review Capitals**	***Review Lowercase**	***Review Numbers**	
17 Activity Pages	**Antonyms** TG2nd pg. 108 PP pg. 63	**Labels & Paragraphs** TG2nd pg. 109 PP pg. 64-65	**Dates, Closing** TG2nd pg. 110 PP pg. 66	**Thank You Letter** TG2nd pg. 111 PP pg. 67	**Letter-Word Fun** TG2nd pg. 112 PP pg. 68	
18 Weeks to follow All Year Activities	***Review CAPITALS**	***Review Lowercase**	**Word Pages**	**Sentences & Paragraphs**	***Review Numbers**	

FAQs

Why aren't there grade levels on your workbooks?
In some instances, we recommend that an older child be taught using a workbook from a lower grade. We don't want the child to feel bad, so we remove the grade level. Thus we focus on the skill, not the grade level.

Why don't you start 6 in the center?
If you teach **b** in the starting corner, children won't reverse it. When children learn **b**, they will naturally add a curve to the top. You shouldn't worry about **b** resembling a **b**—it won't last long.

Why didn't you include x, y, and z when teaching the first group of lowercase letters that are same as capitals?
Letters **x**, **y**, and **z** are used infrequently and have diagonals. We save them until the end because they are more difficult to form and infrequently used.

Why don't you teach q and o with Magic C letters?
The letter **o** is a frequently used letter. We wanted to include it in the first group we taught. Letter **q** is an infrequently used letter and can be confused with **g**, so we save it for the end. When teaching **q** or reviewing lowercase, you may consider these letters as part of the Magic c letter group.

Why don't you teach capitals with a continuous stroke?
When children are young, their motor control is in a constant state of development. Therefore, having them trace back up a line in the initial stages of handwriting can lead to poor letter formation. We can get away with non-retrace of capitals because they are not used as frequently as the lowercase. However, when we move to lowercase, a retrace makes writing faster. We use the skills we develop in capitals to help children at the appropriate time.

Retrace   No Retrace

Why are some of your words are so short?
The words are CVC words: words that have a consonant-vowel-consonant pattern. They are good for young children who are just learning to read and write.

Why don't you do a number check?
Our number check occurs in our kindergarten workbook. If you would like to give a number check to children, you may do it the same way you would check capitals. Use a blank sheet of paper and have the children write all their numbers for you on a single line. You will check for start, steps, and bumping the line.

Why do you illustrate some photos with standard pencils when you only recommend golf-size pencils?
You may transition children to a standard pencil when it feels right for your class. Many first grade teachers make the transition mid year. Writing with a golf size pencil is not a necessity; it is a recommendation. We didn't want all the illustrations to reflect our recommendation because we know that some may choose to stick with standard size pencils.

Why do you sometimes use a Y for a Y and an I for an I?
One is informational, one is instructional. When we teach the letter for handwriting, we want to ensure that the letter is representative of the easiest way to form it. Typically, the other form is used in sentences that will be read, not written. We often use non-HWT forms in our teachers' guides.

Why do you assign multisensory assignments to each letter? Can't you use them interchangeably?
We assign them to help you spread them out throughout your teaching strategies. If you have one that is your favorite or your classes favorite by all means use what is popular. Don't stop there, you might even create a few of your own!

Lowercase Letter Frequency Chart

In 1948, Dr. Edward Dolch published a list of 220 high frequency words. He had word lists for Pre-primer, Primer, First, Second, and Third Grade. To identify high frequency printed words for grades K–2, we used the 177 words on the lists through 2nd grade. Then, we counted how often each letter appears to determine individual letter frequency. This chart shows the letters in order of decreasing frequency. This information was helpful to us in planning our teaching order. Teachers can use this chart to make priority decisions about correcting or reviewing letters.

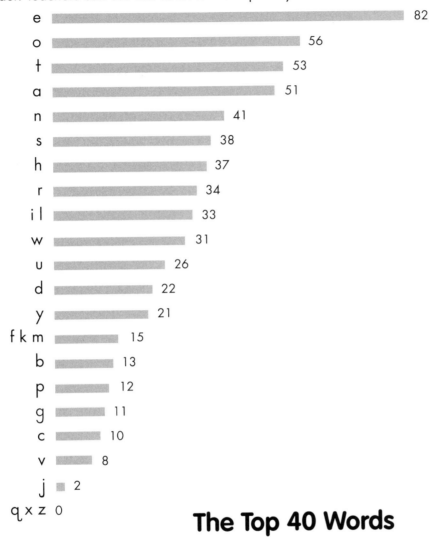

Letter	Frequency
e	82
o	56
t	53
a	51
n	41
s	38
h	37
r	34
i l	33
w	31
u	26
d	22
y	21
f k m	15
b	13
p	12
g	11
c	10
v	8
j	2
q x z	0

The Top 40 Words

Mastering frequently used words is important for fluency. Use this list from the Dolch sight words for practice and review. Be sure to avoid words that use letters you haven't taught yet.

1. the	11. his	21. with	31. be
2. to	12. that	22. up	32. have
3. and	13. she	23. all	33. go
4. he	14. for	24. look	34. we
5. you	15. on	25. is	35. am
6. it	16. they	26. her	36. then
7. of	17. but	27. there	37. little
8. in	18. had	28. some	38. down
9. was	19. at	29. out	39. do
10. said	20. him	30. as	40. can

The FINE Print If we add frequency of v and w, the total is 39; that takes the frequency to the top group. Letter frequency is another reason c o s v w is such an important group.

Capitals, Lowercase Letters, and Numbers

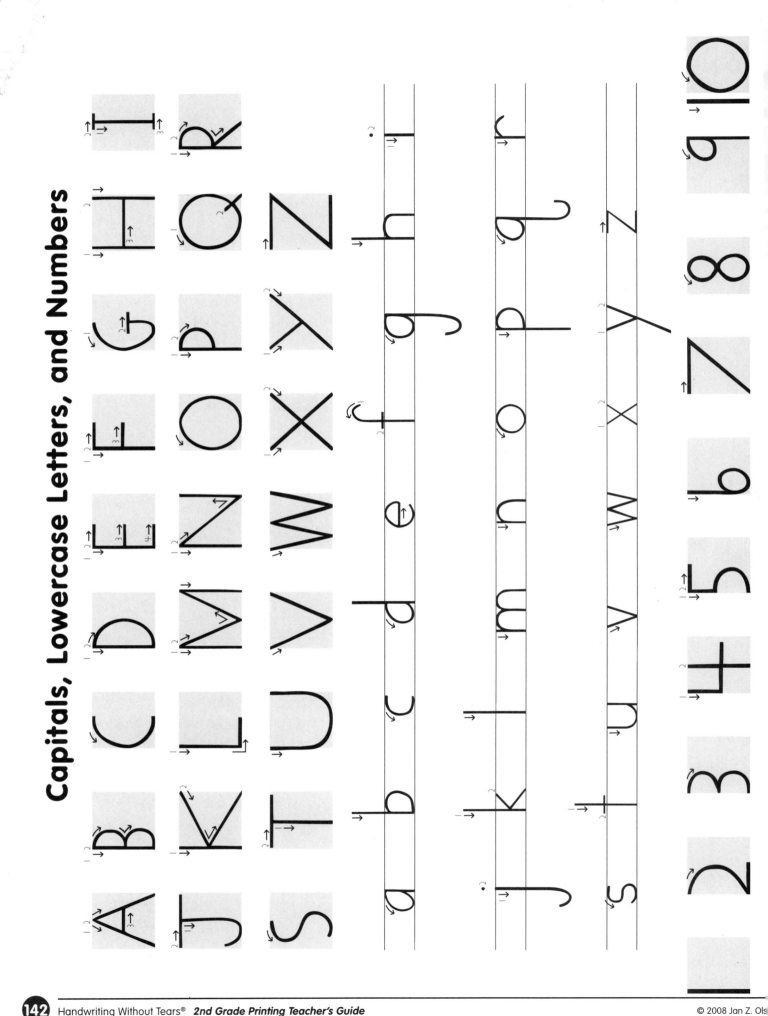